THE MARSHALL CAVENDISH
☆ ☆ ☆ ILLUSTRATED ☆ ☆ ☆
ENCYCLOPEDIA OF
WORLD WAR II

VOLUME 16

THE MARSHALL CAVENDISH
☆ ☆ ☆ ILLUSTRATED ☆ ☆ ☆
ENCYCLOPEDIA OF
WORLD WAR II

Based on the original text by
Lieutenant Colonel Eddy Bauer

CONSULTANT EDITOR

Brigadier General James L. Collins, Jr., U.S.A.
CHIEF OF MILITARY HISTORY,
DEPARTMENT OF THE ARMY

MARSHALL CAVENDISH CORPORATION/NEW YORK

CONTENTS

Editorial Director: Brian Innes
Editor-in-chief; Brigadier Peter Young, D.S.O., M.C., M.A.
Managing Editor: Richard Humble
Editor: Christopher Chant
Art Editor: Jim Bridge

VICTORY IN EUROPE

CHAPTER 138
The fight for Alsace

On October 17, after a fortnight's sustained drive which took the 3rd Algerian Division up the Moselotte as far as Cornimont, General de Lattre decided to change his plans and make a surprise attack on the Belfort gap. But it was important nevertheless that II Corps should not lessen its pressure and allow the enemy to redeploy his forces. The offensive forged ahead, and on November 5 the 3rd Algerian Division (General Guillaume) reached the outskirts of the

Col d'Oderen, more than 3,000 feet high; the opposing enemy forces here included as many as 15 infantry battalions as well as the 169th Division, which had been refitted after its return from Finland.

Such deployment of force was combined with a piece of trickery, whose aim (in de Lattre's own words) was "to give the enemy the impression of total security in Vosges sector. Counterfeit troop movements and the setting up of fictitious H.Q.s were made conspicuous in the area

△ *American infantrymen prepare to attack from trench positions on the outskirts of Colmar. A French-manned tank stands by to give support.*

of Remiremont. At Plombières a detachment of the 5th Armoured Division set up roadsigns, signposted routes and made full use of radio. All this activity drew the attention of enemy spies and if by chance it escaped them the Intelligence agents were there to open their eyes to what was going on." All these indications were corroborated, in General Wiese's mind, by bogus orders and letters, bearing General de Lattre's personal signature, which reached him from reliable sources. The supreme instance of planned deception being "General Directive No. 4", in which the French 1st Army commander announced his intention of simulating troop concentrations in the region of the Doubs to encourage the enemy to withdraw troops from the Vosges.

The attack goes in

At any event the Swiss 2nd Division, in the Porrentruy area, using sound detection apparatus, was able to follow the progressive deployment of powerful artillery on the slopes of the Lomont, for all the discretion the French used in their registration shoots. It is not known whether these indications escaped the notice of the Germans.

De Lattre decided on his plan on October 24: I Corps (General Béthouart) was given the objective of capturing the

▷ *How the Allies cleared Alsace and Lorraine. By the last week of 1944 they had closed up to the Franco-German frontier – but the Germans, on Hitler's orders, continued to hold on in the Colmar pocket.*

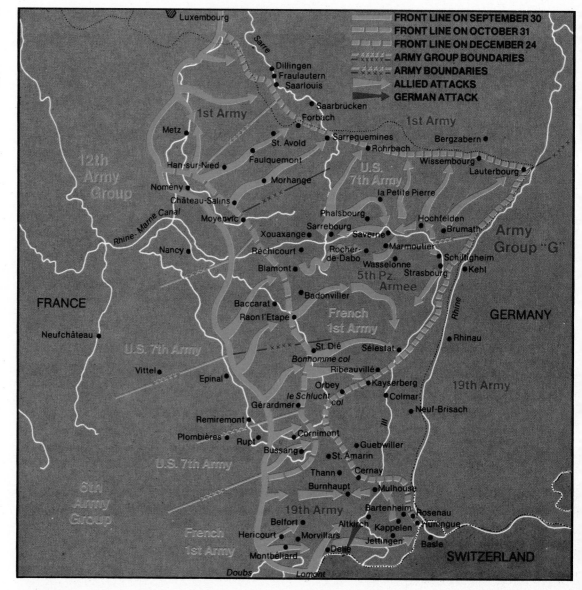

FRONT LINE ON SEPTEMBER 30
FRONT LINE ON OCTOBER 31
FRONT LINE ON DECEMBER 24
xxxxx **ARMY GROUP BOUNDARIES**
xxxx **ARMY BOUNDARIES**
ALLIED ATTACKS
➤ **GERMAN ATTACK**

△ *General Béthouart commanded I Corps in de Lattre's army.*

roads eastwards out of the Belfort gap and simultaneously storming the fortress town. In the event of success, II Corps would join battle, its objective being the Rhine between Huningue and Neuf-Brisach and the line linking Neuf-Brisach–Colmar–Ribeauville. General Devers, whose intention was to push his 7th Army onwards from Saverne to Strasbourg, fully approved the plan drawn up by his immediate subordinate, and allocated him a battalion each of 203-mm guns and 240-mm howitzers, in addition to other weapons.

General Béthouart's first line troops consisted of the 9th Colonial Division (General Magnan) which, reinforced by a Combat Command of the 1st Armoured Division, was to attack between the Swiss frontier and the Doubs (it should be remarked that his Senegalese troops were relieved by Zouaves and Moroccan light infantry, and F.F.I. [French Resistance forces] recruited in the area); also, of the 2nd Moroccan Division, which was given Montbéliard, Héricourt, and Belfort as objectives. The main action would devolve on this latter division, so it was given two Combat Commands, from the 5th Armoured Division.

On the enemy side, LXIV Corps (General Schalk) was deployed on a 30-mile front. On the left was the 338th Division with its back to the Swiss frontier; on the right the 159th, barring the Belfort direction. These were divisions of poor-quality infantry, mainly composed from heterogeneous elements and of differing morale (there was even one deaf battalion).

They were covered by deep, dense anti-tank minefields whose clearance proved to be particularly hazardous, as they were protected by a fearsome array of anti-personnel devices and explosive traps. Requisitioned workers from occupied France – from the Delle district of Belfort – completed the main construc-

tion of a 12-mile anti-tank ditch; this would have constituted a formidable obstacle to the French 1st Army if General de Lattre had deferred the date of his offensive, giving the enemy time to mine it and man its defensive positions.

The attack got under way on November 14 in conditions of sleet, and serious losses were sustained in the minefields. I Corps got a foothold in the enemy positions, but was unable to break through. Two factors favoured the French, however: Lieutenant-General Oschmann, commanding the 338th Division, was killed by a patrol from the 2nd Moroccan Division near the Besançon–Montbéliard road, and his aide-de-camp's briefcase yielded a plan of the division's positions, in addition to copies of several orders. Also, it would appear that for 48 hours, General Wiese's H.Q. minimised the gravity of the French offensive.

At all events, on November 16, the 19th Army received order from Army Group

"G" to fall back on to the Belfort–Delle positions. But its LXIV Corps was so enfeebled that its rearguard was overtaken and mauled by the enemy. The main action took place the following day. On the evening of November 17, the 4th Combat Command (Colonel Schlesser), having adroitly managed to conceal its movement forward from the enemy, took the bridges over the Luzine at Montbéliard by surprise and opened the way for the 2nd Moroccan Division. Near the Swiss frontier, the 9th Division broke through the scanty line of the German 338th Division, enabling Béthouart to unleash the 1st Armoured Division (General du Vigier).

Leaping at the chance, de Lattre the same evening issued a "general order to exploit the situation in full": he issued simultaneous orders to I Corps to head for the Rhine (1st Armoured Division), to reduce the fortress of Belfort (2nd Moroccan Division), and to reincorporate

△ *General Guillaume's Algerians kept up the pressure on the front of II Corps.*

the 5th Armoured Division with a view to attacking Cernay (at a later stage it was his intention to direct it on Colmar and Neuf-Brisach, while the 1st Armoured Division moved towards Sélestat and Strasbourg); at the same time, II Corps would thrust its right forward via Giromagny on Colmar and its left would storm the Col de Bussang and the Col de la Schlucht.

On November 18, the 2nd Moroccan Division, co-operating with the 1st Free French Division (General Brosset) made contact with the defences of Belfort. The 1st Armoured Division, for its part, almost up against the Swiss frontier, crossed the anti-tank ditch mentioned above with barely any loss of momentum and found the bridge over the Allaine at Delle, still intact thanks to the F.F.I. It then took the little town and later that evening destroyed an anti-aircraft unit. The 1st Armoured Division covered more than 18 miles in the course of the day.

The French reach the Rhine first . . .

The following day the same division covered more than 25 miles. The 3rd Combat Command (Colonel Caldairou) led the column. During its race to the Rhine it encountered only scant resistance and at 1700 hours, after crossing the Ill, it passed through Jettingen, only eight miles from its objective. "Then", wrote de Lattre, "the advance became a charge. At full speed, a detachment commanded by Lieutenant de Loisy, including a group of Sherman tanks and a section of the 1st Zouaves dashed eastwards, Helfranzkirch, Kappeln, Bartenheim . . . Occasional burst of machine gun fire at isolated enemy. Barely four miles more. Rosenau: 15 bewildered prisoners. A quarter of a mile to go. A screen of trees . . . The Rhine! . . . What a moment to be alive! 1830 hours on November 19, 1944, what humiliations avenged! First of all the Allied armies, the French 1st Army reached the banks of the Rhine."

True, to the south of Belfort, the enemy, though thrown back sharply on one flank near Morvillars, was offering stubborn resistance to attacks from the 9th Colonial Division. At the same time the roads between Montbéliard and Morvillars, and Montbéliard and Fesche-

General Alphonse Juin was born in Algeria in 1888. He went to the Saint Cyr military academy in 1909 and passed out top of his year— a year which included de Gaulle. He served with distinction in World War I and was awarded the Légion d'Honneur, and between the wars he served in Morocco, proving himself an able diplomat and strategist. On the eve of World War II he reached general rank, and in 1940 he was captured by the Germans while commanding a division of the French 1st Army. He was released after the Armistice at the express request of Marshal Pétain. Having refused a post in the Vichy Government, he then succeeded Weygand as C.-in-C. North Africa. Divided between his loyalty as a soldier and his dislike of the Vichy Government, he did not assert himself in this post until after the Clark-Darlan agreement of 1942, when he became an excellent defender of the Allied cause, fighting Rommel in the Western Desert. He was made a General in 1942, and later he commanded the French Expeditionary Corps which achieved such brilliant results in Italy, from Cassino to Rome. In 1944 he was promoted Chief-of-Staff of France's National Defence Committee, and raised fresh troops for the liberation of France, in which he commanded four divisions.

l'Eglise was so crowded with vehicles that it proved impossible to clear it for the 5th Armoured Division in time for its new assignment (given in the orders of November 17). Nevertheless, on the 20th, the 3rd Combat Command of the 1st Armoured Division took Mulhouse, and just missed capturing General Wiese; in its wake, Colonel Gruss, at the head of the 1st Combat Command, struck at Altkirch from Seppois-le-Haut. Finally, on the same day, the fortress town of Belfort was completely invested.

Balck counter-attacks

At Army Group "G" H.Q., General Balck was in a quandary. On the one hand, Hitler had given him orders to counter-attack the French 1st Army, cutting off those of its elements that had reached the Rhine; on the other, the American 7th Army offensive in the Saverne sector was likely at any moment to lead to sever the line of his 1st and 19th Armies. Hence on November 20 he suggested to Rundstedt that Schmidt von Knobelsdorf be buttressed with reinforcements intended for the counter-attack, allowing that Wiese could be withdrawn north of Mulhouse. But, characteristically, Hitler was intractable and Balck had no alternative but to set about making the–in his view unworkable–plan work.

The 198th Division was withdrawn from the Saint Dié–Gérardmer sector, brought back over the Schlucht to Dannemarie, from where it launched a counter-attack on November 21 towards the Swiss frontier. At its point of departure, it was reinforced with the 106th Panzer Brigade, equipped with *Jagdpanthers* and Pzkw IV's. On its left it had the support of the 30th S.S. Division, composed of Russian renegades. Torrential rain prevented the French seeing the troop movements behind the enemy lines, as the 198th Division took up position. Furthermore, for the reasons already given, General de Lattre had not been reinforced by the 5th Armoured Division in the time required by his order of November 17. So it was that Schiel broke the weak link in the French lines south of Dannemarie and cut the road, between Delle and Seppois, which constituted the 1st Armoured Division's supply line.

However, on November 22, the 198th Division was itself outflanked by the 5th Armoured Division and the 9th Colonial Division and subjected to a tremendous artillery battering. Forty-eight hours later, General Béthouart, at the cost of furious effort and appreciable losses, cut it in two along the line of the Delle–Seppois road, and the 1st Armoured Division's communications were restored. The greater part of the 308th and 326th Grenadier Regiments fought their last battle with their backs to the Swiss frontier. The ordeal was over by the end of the afternoon of November 24. The

German square made an heroic last stand.

19th Army caught

The issue here was still undecided when on November 22 de Lattre unleashed II Corps in a manoeuvre that elevated the whole battle from the tactical to the strategic level. On the same day the 2nd Moroccan Division won a fierce struggle to capture the fort and village of Giromagny, and on November 25 the fortress of Belfort was wholly in its possession. This made it possible to surround the German 19th Army by a pincer movement, with II Corps from Belfort moving to join I Corps attacking from a line between Mulhouse and Altkirch, westwards and

△ *A house-to-house search for German snipers in Niederbronn just after its capture.*

Freiburg 57 km
Banzenheim 19 km
Hüningen-St Ludwig 38 km
Altheim 8 km
Kolmar 39 km
Kingersheim 5 km
Müllheim

△ *A Stuart light tank of the French 1st Army clatters through liberated Mulhouse.*

south-westwards. But in the meantime de Lattre had to release his excellent 1st Free French Division, which had received orders to go and clear the Gironde sector of enemy forces. In addition, de Lattre again found himself short of munitions. Hence it cost considerable effort for General de Monsabert to force a way through and, on November 28, to link up with his comrade Béthouart.

The liquidation of the pocket so formed round the 159th, 198th, and 338th Divisions brought the number of prisoners taken by the French in this action to more than 17,000. More than 10,000 German dead, 120 guns, and 60 tanks, some of them *Jagdpanthers,* littered the battlefield. The French 1st Army losses were 1,440 killed and missing, 4,500 wounded, and 1,694 evacuated with severe frostbite. Among the dead was the intrepid General Brosset, killed in a jeep accident on November 20. General Garbay succeeded him in command of the 1st Free French Division.

So it was that at the beginning of December, for lack of two or three additional divisions, the 1st Army halted its thrust forward on a line linking the Huningue Canal, a point north of Mul-

house, Thann, Saint Amarin, and the Col de la Schlucht.

7th Army held up

On the 6th Army Group's left, the American 7th Army, still under General Patch, after an equally promising start experienced similar frustration for similar reasons.

General Devers had given it the job of liberating the plain of Alsace between, and including, Strasbourg and Wissembourg, and of throwing the enemy back across the Rhine. Already, on October 31, the French 2nd Armoured Division had taken the initiative of forcing the Meurthe and pushing beyond Baccarat, so that by D-day, November 13, the American XIII Corps, which had been responsible for the main action, held a line in front of Badonviller, Blâmont, and Réchicourt. Opposing it, the 708th and 553rd Divisions, on the left flank of the German 1st Army, stood across the Saverne gap. General Haislip, commanding XV Corps, had the 79th and 44th Infantry Divisions up, with the French

2nd Armoured Division to exploit the breakthrough, which came on November 16.

Leclerc's charge

To this effect, General Leclerc had been preparing his plan on a huge relief map. On November 10 he summoned Colonel de Langlade, commanding one of his three Combat Commands, and told him: "You must move down into Alsace at top speed... and surprise the Boches beyond possibility of recovery . . . You won't go via Sarrebourg and Saverne, it'll be Dio's job to try that way. All the main roads will be riddled with obstructions . . . you'd be stuck somewhere in the middle... You will see to it to find a way through here . . ."

Thereupon, with a pointer he indicated a network of minor roads starting out from Cirey, twisting and turning in all directions, crossing the White Sarre and the Red Sarre before reaching the Rethel crossroads, six miles south-east of Sarrebourg, deep in the southern spurs of the Vosges.

And Leclerc went on: "Once at Rethel, we'll see, but you'll have to do all you can to take the road following the Dabo; it's the shortest way to drop down onto Wasselonne or Marmoutier in the plain of Alsace. The enemy will be expecting you along the Saverne roads, he won't think of your taking the Dabo, it simply wouldn't occur to him that an armoured division could come through on these mountain tracks . . . All right?"

General de Langlade, as he now is, confesses he felt somewhat aghast at the itinerary he had been given, wondering how his 32-ton Shermans would manage the steep gradients, the curves, and the hairpin bends; he was thinking too that such terrain would be ideal for enemy ambushes and that in any event the torrential and persistent rain of the previous days might have made the route all but impassable.

But Leclerc went on: "Yes, I know, such an itinerary must seem to you madness . . . But it's the right one and will bring you success. Anyway, I'm not asking you to follow every detail of my plan and please don't discuss it. If I've entrusted you with this cavalry mission which seems so fraught with danger, it's precisely because so far you

have always carried out my orders swiftly and to the letter. All I ask is for you to go ahead and this time surpass yourself . . ."

Once at Cirey-sur-Vezouse, Leclerc split his force into two parts. On the right, Combat Command "L", incorporating Lieutenant-Colonel de Guillebon's Combat Command "W", set off on the itinerary assigned to it on November 19, with the order: "Go hell for leather!" Matching the deed to the letter, Major Massu, sticking to the Dabo, came out into the plain of Alsace in torrential rain at 0930 on November 21, closely followed by Combat Command "W", which at the end of the day reached and liberated Marmoutier, on the Saverne–Strasbourg road.

On the left, overtaking the 44th Division, Combat Command "D" (Colonel Dio) had the mission of pushing on towards Sarrebourg, Phalsbourg, and Saverne, to the north of the *Route Nationale* 4: so doing it crossed the Marne–Rhine Canal at Xouaxange by a bridge that was still standing, thanks to the local lock-keeper who kept plying the sappers whose job it was to destroy it with *vin gris*. Major Quiliquini was stopped at Phalsbourg, but his frontal assault on the 553rd Division enabled Colonel Rouvillois to outflank the enemy, finding a way round by la Petite Pierre; on the way, he had a go at the 316th Division, and during the evening of November 21 he too had reached the plain of Alsace north-east of Saverne.

The next day, early in the afternoon, Combat Command "L" stormed Saverne from the rear, and Massu, who led the attack, achieved such an element of surprise that, among the 800 prisoners the little town's capture yielded, figured Lieutenant-General Bruhn, commanding the 553rd Division. A few hours later, coming at the strong but west-facing defences of Phalsbourg from the east, Minjonnet's right-hand column from Combat Command "L" re-established communication between the 2nd Armoured Division and XV Corps along the Saverne–Sarrebourg road.

"Thus", writes General de Langlade, "one November evening, Saverne was captured; the Saverne gap, blocked at Phalsbourg by solidly entrenched enemy forces, fell into our hands; liaison between American units (44th Division) and Dio's Combat Command 'D' was all but complete again. The way to Strasbourg was open."

△ *General Devers, whose 6th Army Group held the extreme right of the Allied front in north-west Europe.*

△ *General Patch. His 7th Army operated on the left of 6th Army Group, with de Lattre's army on its right.*

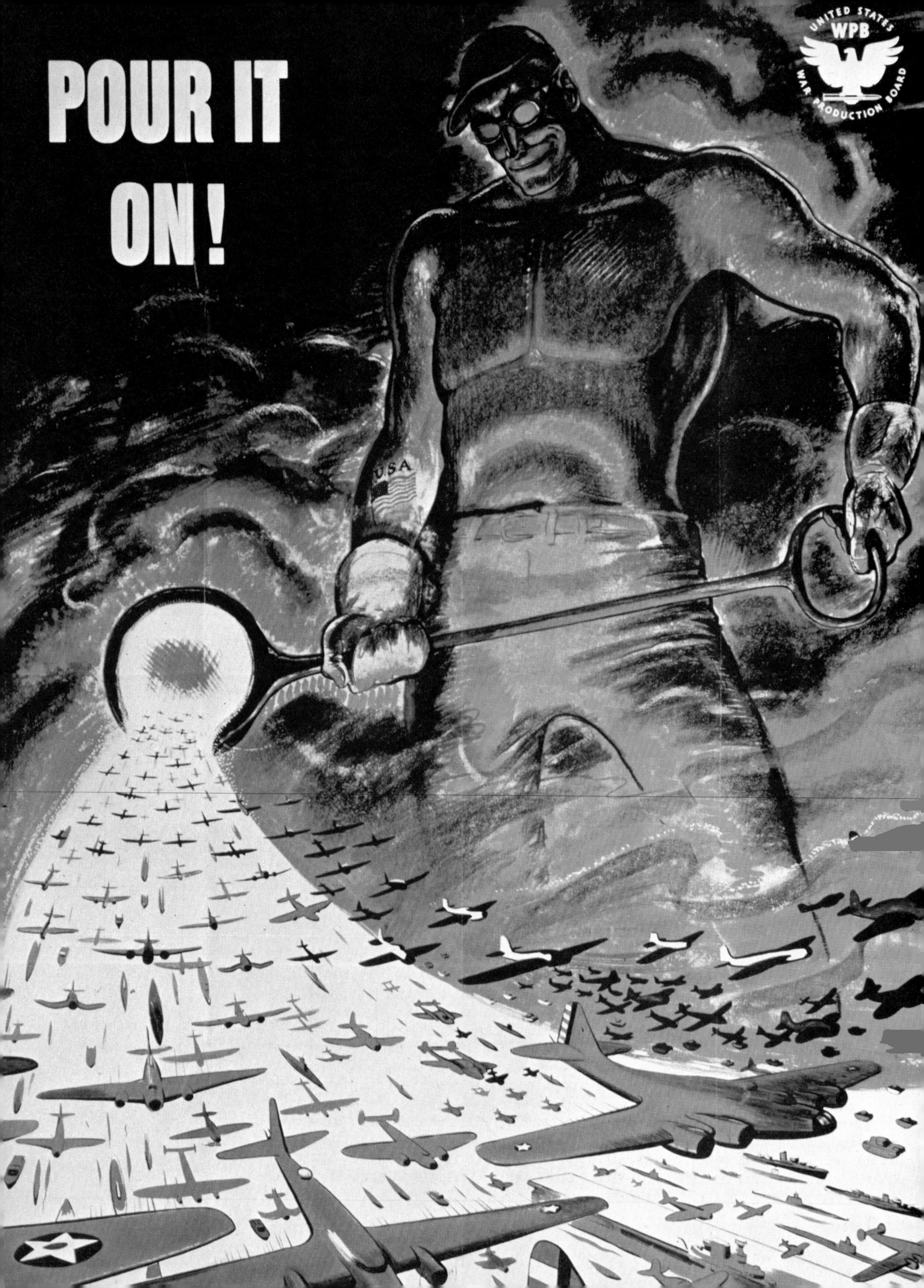
POUR IT
ON!
UNITED STATES
WPB
WAR PRODUCTION BOARD
USA

AMERICA'S WAR EFFORT

By the end of 1944 the contribution to the war effort of "The Great Arsenal of Democracy" was already legendary. It was seen in manpower. It was seen in financial aid. It was seen in munitions production. And it was the biggest single factor in the Allies' favour as they ground painfully eastward towards the Rhine and the decisive invasion of Germany.

In the Battle of the Atlantic the vast output of America's shipyards had been as potent a weapon in the defeat of the U-boats as sonar detection, air cover, or the depth charge. American transports, shipped to Russia via the agonising "blackout" route to Murmansk and Archangel, had put the Red Army on wheels for the first time in its history – a fact freely and

generously admitted by Soviet commanders. And the financial air of Lend-Lease constituted the war chest of the Allied war effort against Germany and Japan.

Axis propaganda made ceaseless play against the corroding power of the American dollar. This was hardly surprising. Even without the contributions made by American banks, 100 billion

1. *The colossus of American war production. Thirty years before World War II, Sir Edward Grey had likened the U.S.A. to a gigantic boiler, with limitless energy once the fire was lighted beneath it. Now his prophecy was proved true with a vengeance.*
2. *Fuselage components for Flying Fortress heavy bombers on the production line.*

3. Sonorous patriotism with pious religious undertones: an appeal for 100 per cent national war effort in the factory and in the field.

4. For the benefit of the worker. Despite the agreement of the unions not to strike during the war, there were 15,000 work stoppages in the United States between 1941 and 1945. Congress was forced to retaliate by passing an act requiring unions to observe a 30-day pause before striking, and empowering the President to seize striking war plants.

5. Mass-production in the shipyards: "pre-fab" American transports take shape.

6. The intense tempo of the American warship-building schedule. As one sub-chaser takes to the water, the keel assembly for its replacement is lowered into position on the stocks.

Strong in the strength of the Lord we who fight in the people's cause will never stop until that cause is won

dollars' worth of war bonds were bought by American investors. U.S. war-time taxes netted 138 billion dollars; and the American national debt rocketed from 49 billion dollars in 1941 to 259 billion dollars in 1945.

Yet the American war machine did not function with 100 per cent efficiency. Labour disputes remained a problem. The main unions undertook not to strike while the war was still in progress – yet between 1941 and 1945 there were 15,000 work stoppages. Governmental retaliation was needed, and Congress passed an act which required the unions to observe a 30-day respite before striking. And the President was given powers to seize striking war plants.

Sacrifice at home was lower than any of the Allied powers. This was inevitable. The war was so far away. Rationing was imposed in the U.S.A., but with nothing like as much severity as in Britain. Even so, war bonds, salvage, and economy drives remained a constant feature of life in war-time America and enabled the civilian to feel – in the World War I catchphrase – that he was "doing his bit" for democracy and the western way of life.

5

7. *Bizarre silhouettes against the sky: contributions at a salvage rubber collection centre.*

8. *Reminiscent of the British "saucepans to Spitfires" campaign—contributions to the nation's aluminium recovery programme are solicited. As in Britain, few were churlish enough to point out that brand-new aluminium pots and pans were still on sale in the shops.*

9. *A typical war bonds appeal. Results were good: even without the contributions of the big banks, $100 billion's worth of war bonds was purchased by investors.*

7

8

ALUMINUM
HOT OR COLD
NEW-OR OLD
ITS GOOD AS GOLD

The manoeuvre to take Strasbourg began on November 23 at 0645 hours and involved four routes; two were taken by Colonel de Guillebon and two by Colonel de Langlade. Kehl was the final objective. Three hours later, three of the four French columns came upon the outlying forts, interconnected by an anti-tank ditch. The fourth (Rouvillois's subsidiary group) which had taken the itinerary Hochfelden–Brumath–Schiltigheim, surprised the defence by emerging from this unexpected direction, and at 1010 hours sent the agreed coded message: *"Tissu est dans iode"* (fabric in iodine, or Rouvillois in Strasbourg). It was soon followed by the remainder of Combat Com-

CHAPTER 139
Colmar pocket

mand "L" and all of "W", but was unable to prevent the destruction of the Kehl bridge. Amidst the confusion, superbly stage-managed on the telephone system by 2nd Lieutenant Braun, Colonel de Langlade's Intelligence officer, issuing bogus orders to the enemy staffs, resistance was throttled in the course of the afternoon and at 1800 hours, the French flag was seen flying at the top of the cathedral spire, telling Strasbourg and the world that General Leclerc had kept the promise he had made at Kufra Oasis on March 1, 1941, when the least partisan observers had considered Hitler's victory assured.

In the afternoon of November 25th, Lieutenant-General Vaterrodt, commanding the garrison, and his second-in-command, Major-General Uttersprungen, who had sought refuge in Fort Ney,

▽ *French armour moves up on the Colmar front.*

surrendered to a detachment of the 2nd Armoured Division. So ended General Leclerc's amazing exploit.

Eighty-two days' misery: that, in General de Langlade's words, was to be the lot of the 2nd Armoured Division on the morrow of its brilliant victory. Without necessarily disagreeing with this opinion, it should, however, be observed that the same run of bad luck afflicted the American 7th Army, indeed the whole of the 6th Army Group.

After cutting through the solid front formed by the enemy 1st and 19th Armies, General Patch threw his VI and XV Corps forward towards the German fron-

◁ ◁ *A farm building blazes near Sarrebourg.*
◁ *A bag of German officers captured at Saverne.*
▽ *The tricolour flies in a Belfort street as the French march in – hugging the walls against possible ambush.*

On patrol with American ski
paratroops in the French Alps.
△ On the move in line-ahead.
△▷ A practice mortar shoot.
▷ An injured soldier gets
treatment from the "medic"
dropped with every detachment.
▷▷ The patrol moves out from
base.

△ *Lieutenant-General Vaterrodt, who surrendered Strasbourg to Leclerc.*
▷ *French gunners in Strasbourg.*

tier in accordance with his orders to provide support for the 3rd Army in its attack on the *Westwall*. On his right, VI Corps, now commanded by Major-General Edward H. Brooks, following General Truscott's appointment as commander of the American 5th Army in Italy, got its 79th Division to Lauterbourg on December 6, while the 45th was attacking the Siegfried Line parallel to Bergzabern, both of them biting deep into the German defensive system. On his left, XV Corps was hammering away at the fortifications in the area of Bitche, the only section of the Maginot Line to play a rôle in 1944. It had reduced them when the Ardennes offensive forced it to let go its hold.

At Strasbourg, the American 3rd Division (VI Corps) had relieved the French 2nd Armoured Division which, in company with the American 36th and 103rd Divisions, tried to prevent the enemy establishing new positions round Colmar. Here General Patch was endeavouring to do two things at the same time: effect a break-through in the *Westwall* between the Rhine and the Saar, and clear the enemy from the left bank of the Rhine above Strasbourg. This double assign-

ment was given him by General Devers who, in calling for two divergent operations, was doing no more than conform to instructions from S.H.A.E.F. where the enemy's capacity for resistance was not fully realised.

However, on December 2 H.Q. 6th Army Group took the American 7th Army off the Colmar assignment and gave it to the French 1st Army, at the same time allocating the 36th Division and the 2nd Armoured Division. This was indeed a logical decision, but one that resolved nothing, since the switch produced no reinforcements. And de Lattre, as we know, had been reluctantly obliged to part with his 1st Free French Division and was further expecting, according to orders received from Paris, to lose his 1st Armoured Division, which was to be sent to Royan.

Then again, at Vittel, General Devers's Intelligence staff took an optimistic view: the stiffening of enemy resistance in Alsace was recognised, but attributed to O.K.W.'s concern not to pull its troops back from the left bank of the Rhine until it had had ample time to provide for the defence of the right bank of the river.

The German Pzkw VI Tiger II heavy tank

Weight: 68.65 tons.
Crew: 5.
Armament: one 8.8-cm KwK 43 gun with 80 rounds, plus one 7.92-mm MG 42 and two 7.92-mm MG 34 machine guns with 5,850 rounds.
Armour: hull front 100-mm, sides and rear 80-mm, and belly 40-mm; superstructure front 150-mm, sides and rear 80-mm, and decking 40-mm; turret front 185-mm, sides and rear 80-mm and roof 40-mm.
Engine: one Maybach HL 230 P30 inline, 600-hp.
Speed: 25.7 mph on roads and 12 mph cross-country.
Range: 106 miles on roads and 75 miles cross-country.
Length: 33 feet 8 inches.
Width: 12 feet 3⅝ inches with battle tracks, 10 feet 8¾ inches with narrow tracks.
Height: 10 feet 1⅝ inches.

Hitler and Colmar

In fact, this view was quite mistaken. On the contrary, in the middle of all this, Hitler dismissed General Balck and put General Wiese and his 19th Army under a new command known as *"Oberrhein"*, which he entrusted to *Reichsführer*-S.S. Heinrich Himmler; and far from proceeding to evacuate the Colmar bridgehead he set about reconstituting its defence, which he did with great success.

Carrying out the orders that had come from the 6th Army Group, General de Lattre incorporated the two divisions he had been allotted as well as the 3rd Algerian Division, the Moroccan troops, and the 4th Combat Command (5th Armoured Division) in II Corps and ordered it to attack the north-west front of the pocket, from a line linking the Col du Bonhomme, Ribeauville, Sélestat, and Rhinau. At the same time, I Corps had orders to attack from a line between

Mulhouse and Thann, both corps being given Neuf-Brisach as their objective. We drew attention earlier to the reasons for the reverse suffered by Béthouart around December 10. And Monsabert, for all his dash, had troops that were too few and too battle-weary to bring him greater success. The energy he displayed enabled him to batter the enemy front but not break it, as his orders required; in arctic conditions, he managed to capture Orbey and Kayserberg, taking 5,568 prisoners, but his own losses were heavy and on December 19 he was ordered to take up a defensive position on the line he had reached.

In this battle, the French 1st Army, as General de Lattre de Tassigny remarks, was at a disadvantage in that the Wehrmacht's Panthers and *Jagdpanthers* outclassed the Shermans and Allied tank destroyers with disastrous consequences. But apart from this, morale on the German side had been greatly strengthened. The diminished success of the Colmar offensive caused some friction between de

▽ *Algerian troops dug in, with Hellcats at the ready in the background.*

Lattre and Devers, the first asking the second for two further divisions and the second replying that the other Allied armies were managing well enough without receiving reinforcements. It would seem that in drawing this comparison, General Devers quite failed to appreciate the factor of air cover, which operated very much to the advantage of Simpson, Hodges, Patton, and even Patch, while his French subordinate was cruelly deprived. Apart from that, neither Devers nor General Eisenhower even had the two divisions requested by de Lattre available to give him. The supply of reinforcements from across the Atlantic had been speeded up, but in early December 1944 S.H.A.E.F. had only 66 divisions immediately available, so that its main reserves were barely sufficient.

Not enough manpower

And this leads us to draw the following conclusion on the whole episode. In every army in the world, before the appearance of atomic weapons, it was an article of faith that the commander-in-chief's power of decision depends on the number of men at his disposal. Thus, on the eve of the German counter-attack of March 21, 1918, behind the 119 divisions at the front, Haig and Pétain had 62 in reserve. In the present instance, this was far from the case. So Eisenhower should not be blamed, as so often he is, for not exercising greater authority over his immediate subordinates, since he lacked the means that would have enabled him to enforce his decisions.

This situation led to defeat at Arnhem, qualified success or failure on the Rur. As for the victories won on fronts which Montgomery would have preferred to leave inactive, they were not exploited for want of the ten or so divisions that would have allowed Patton, Patch, and de Lattre to attack the *Westwall* between the Moselle and the Rhine, before Hitler moved in the Ardennes.

▽ *General de Lattre de Tassigny salutes his tank crews.*

▷ By the end of 1944 de Lattre's troops had cleared Alsace, but the Colmar pocket was still holding out.
▽ A French Stuart passes a rank of recently-captured Germans, waiting with their hands up to be marched off to the P.O.W. pen.

CHAPTER 140

The Ardennes gamble

Previous page: *The scene of the notorious "Malmédy massacre" at the crossroads of the hamlet of Baugnez. Here, on the afternoon of December 17, 1944, the advance guard of Kampfgruppe "Peiper" ran into Battery B, U.S. 285th Field Artillery Observation Battalion and captured some 150 men. A Rumanian S.S. trooper fired at one of the prisoners, and this sparked off the massacre. Of more than 150 prisoners in the roadside meadow, 84 were killed and the rest gravely wounded.*
△ *A bridge blown by American engineers erupts up into the sky as the Allies pull back.*

It is now well known that the "Battle of the Bulge", the offensive often known as Rundstedt's, was in reality forced upon him, and that the rôle played by O.B. West in the attack begun on December 16 was limited to that of passing on to Army Group "B" the instructions of Hitler, Keitel, and Jodl at O.K.W.

It was quite clear to Rundstedt, Model, and even to Sepp Dietrich, that the objectives assigned to Operation *"Herbstnebel"* ("Autumn Fog") were far too ambitious for the Wehrmacht's limited capabilities, and they tried to convince the Führer of this. On the other hand they agreed with him–and history bears out their judgement–that if the Third Reich was not to be annihilated in less than six months, they would have to go over to the offensive, the Western Front being the only theatre where this might be possible. Italy was not vital to the Western Allies, even if the terrain and the season had made such an operation there successful; and in the East, it was generally agreed that they would not be able to force a decisive result. According to Major-General Gehlen's calculations, Stalin had something like 520 infantry divisions and more than 300 armoured and mechanised brigades

at his command, and so could lose up to 30 divisions, or retreat up to 150 miles, without suffering a decisive defeat. In any case, what could be the advantage to the Germans of advancing once more to the Dniepr or the Dvina, if in the meantime the Western Allies broke through the *Westwall* and occupied the Ruhr and Saar basins?

Total secrecy

The German chiefs thus agreed unanimously on a counter-offensive in the West, being fully aware of the logistical difficulties and man-power shortage by which Eisenhower was being plagued. However, there was deep disagreement between the Führer and his front-line generals on how far to carry the offensive. Hitler maintained that they ought to go all out, and inflict on Eisenhower a defeat as crushing as that suffered by Gamelin when the Panzer divisions had pushed through to the Somme estuary in 1940. And the fact that the Ardennes mountains were so lightly held seemed to provide him with an opportunity identical to the one he had exploited in May 1940–

we now know that he did in fact send to Liegnitz for the documents pertaining to *"Fall Gelb"*. The plan was being prepared at H.Q. in absolute secrecy–and neither Rundstedt nor Model knew of it. Three armies were to take part: the newly formed 6th S.S. *Panzerarmee,* commanded by Colonel-General Dietrich; the 5th *Panzerarmee* under General Hasso von Manteuffel, which was withdrawn from the Aix-la-Chapelle front (neither Model nor Rundstedt was informed of the rôle it was going to play); and the 7th Army, under General Brandenberger, which was then in the Eifel sector.

According to O.K.W.'s plan, the 5th and 6th *Panzerarmee* were to get to the Meuse in 48 hours; after this Sepp Dietrich, crossing the river north of Liège, would aim for Antwerp, via Saint Truiden and Aarschot, whilst Manteuffel, crossing the river on both sides of Namur, would aim for Brussels. The 7th Army would pivot round at Echternach and thus cover the operation against any Allied counter-attack coming from the south. With Manteuffel and Dietrich intercepting their communications at Namur and Antwerp, the whole of the Allied 21st Army Group, and most of the 12th Army Group, would be attacked on two fronts and annihilated, with the destruction of 37 of the 64 divisions that Eisenhower deployed at that time.

Counter-proposal

On October 24, Lieutenant-Generals Krebs and Westphal, chiefs-of-staff of Army Group "B" and of O.B. West respectively, had an interview with the Führer, who informed them of the plan which he had conceived, and whose execution was provisionally fixed for November 25. Both at Koblenz and at Field-Marshal Model's H.Q., the *Führerbefehl* had been severely criticised by those who would have to carry it out, as– and Krebs and Westphal had already hinted as much on a previous visit to O.K.W.–the plan bore no relationship to the resources being made available to them. Since, however, they were both in favour of a strategic counter-attack, on November 3 they submitted a counter-proposition to Hitler, better suited to the capabilities of Army Group "B", and called the "little solution" *(kleine Lösung)*.

Instead of embarking on the very risky task of recapturing Antwerp, they suggested that it would be better to take advantage of the salient that the American 1st and 9th Armies had created in the *Westwall,* east and north-east of Aix-la-Chapelle, and envelop it in a pincer movement, enabling Dietrich to break out of the Roermond region and Manteuffel out of the Eifel region. If such an attack were completely successful, 20 Allied divisions would be destroyed and Model could then perhaps exploit Bradley's defeat and strike out for Antwerp.

As can be seen, Model, who had conceived this plan, and Rundstedt, who had forwarded it to O.K.W. with his approval, looked upon the operation as a mere sortie, just as the commander of a besieged 18th Century fortress would suddenly make a night attack on the besieging forces, forcing them to start their siege preparations anew. But such an operation gained only a few weeks' respite and, sooner or later, unless help was forthcoming from elsewhere, surrender would be inevitable. Understandably then, Hitler angrily rejected such a solution, for what he needed was not a short respite,

▽ *British paratroopers advance cautiously through the ruins of a factory in their successful operations further north.*

but a decisive military victory in the West. So, as early as November 1, he had written at the head of his orders to O.B. West, that "the intention, the organisation, and the objective of this offensive are irrevocable". On receiving the counter-proposition of Model and Rundstedt, he got Jodl to reply within 24 hours that "the Führer has decided that the operation is irrevocably decided, down to its last details".

However, none of the H.Q. staff had solved any of the difficulties which the men in field command of the operation had felt obliged to point out. As Rundstedt explained on October 25, 1945, whilst being interrogated by Major Shulman of Canadian 1st Army Intelligence:

"When I was first told about the proposed offensive in the Ardennes, I protested against it as vigorously as I could. The forces at our disposal were much, much too weak for such far-reaching objectives. It was only up to one to obey. It was a nonsensical operation, and the most stupid part of it was the setting of Antwerp as the target. If

▽ American vehicles captured by the Germans in Belgium. By the skilful and daring use of such captured equipment, the Germans hoped to sow distrust and worry in the Allied rear areas.

△ *A section of U.S. infantry moves up into a Belgian village under cover of a Sherman tank.*

we reached the Meuse we should have got down on our knees and thanked God – let alone try to reach Antwerp."

Hitler paid no more heed to Sepp Dietrich than he had to Model and Rundstedt, his only concession being to put back the date of the offensive from November 25, first to December 10, then to December 16. He also agreed to Manteuffel's suggestion to replace the three-hour artillery barrage that he had ordered by an artillery attack of only 45 minutes.

The forces assemble

The operation forced O.K.W. to redeploy its western forces. To free Model of any worries concerning his right wing, an Army Group "H" was organised, responsible for operations between the North Sea and Roermond, and commanded by Colonel-General Student, who relinquished his 1st Parachute Army to General Schlemm.

The 15th Army relieved the 5th *Panzerarmee* on the Roer (or Rur in Germany), being relieved in turn between the North Sea and Nijmegen by a 25th Army under the command of General Christiansen.

According to General von Manteuffel,

at 0530 hours on December 16, 21 German divisions of all types launched their attack on the American line between Monschau and Echternach, on a 90-mile front. From north to south, the forces involved were:

1. 6th S.S. *Panzerarmee:* LXVII Corps (General Hitzfeld), with the 272nd and 326th *Volksgrenadier* Divisions; I S.S. Panzer Corps (General Priess), with the 277th and 12th *Volksgrenadier,* 3rd Parachute, and 1st and 12th S.S. Panzer Divisions; and II S.S. Panzer Corps (General Bittrich), with the 2nd and 9th S.S. Panzer Divisions.

2. 5th *Panzerarmee:* LXVI Corps (General Lucht), with the 18th and 62nd *Volksgrenadier* Divisions; LVIII Panzer Corps (General Krüger), with the 116th Panzer and 560th *Volksgrenadier* Divisions; and XLVII Panzer Corps (General von Lüttwitz), with the 2nd Panzer, Panzer-*"Lehr",* and 26th *Volksgrenadier* Divisions.

3. 7th Army: LXXXV Corps (General Kniess), with the 5th Parachute and 352nd *Volksgrenadier* Divisions; and LXXX Corps (General Beyer), with the 276th and 212nd *Volksgrenadier* Divisions.

It should be noted that although the four *Waffen*-S.S. Panzer divisions had been brought up to full strength, with a total of

The German *Panzerjäger* Tiger or *Jagdtiger* tank destroyer

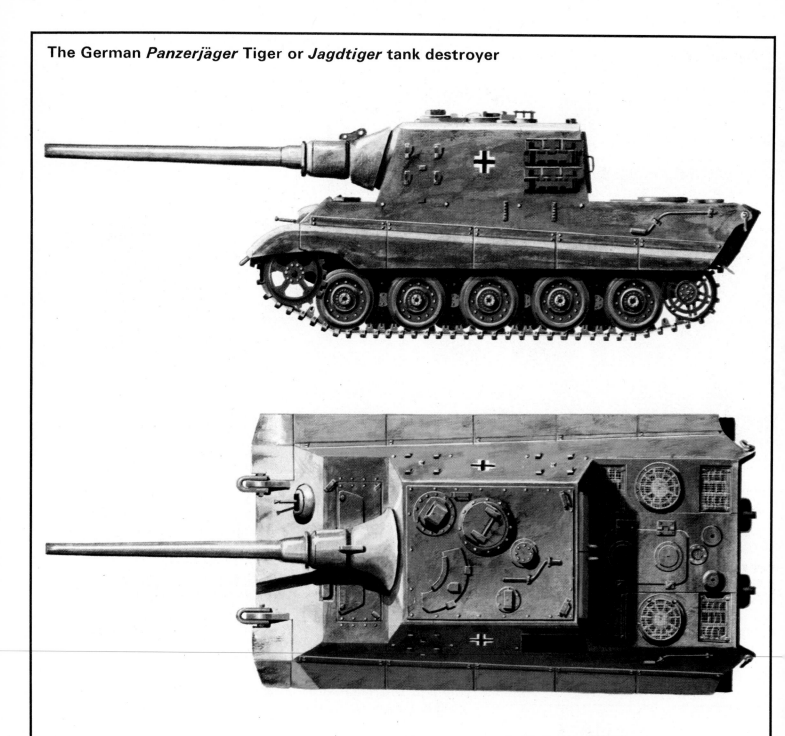

Weight: 70.6 tons.
Crew: 6.
Armament: one 12.8-cm PaK 80 L/55 gun with 38 rounds and one MG 34 machine gun.
Armour: hull front 100-mm, sides and rear 80-mm, and belly and decking 40-mm; superstructure front 250-mm, sides and rear 80-mm, and roof 40-mm.
Engine: one Maybach HL 230 P30 inline, 700-hp.
Speed: 23.6 mph on roads and 12 mph cross-country.
Range: 100 miles on roads and 75 miles cross-country.
Length: 34 feet 11$\frac{1}{2}$ inches.
Width: 11 feet 10$\frac{3}{4}$ inches with battle tracks, and 10 feet 8$\frac{3}{4}$ inches with narrow tracks.
Height: 9 feet 3 inches.

The American/British Sherman M4A4/VC Firefly tank

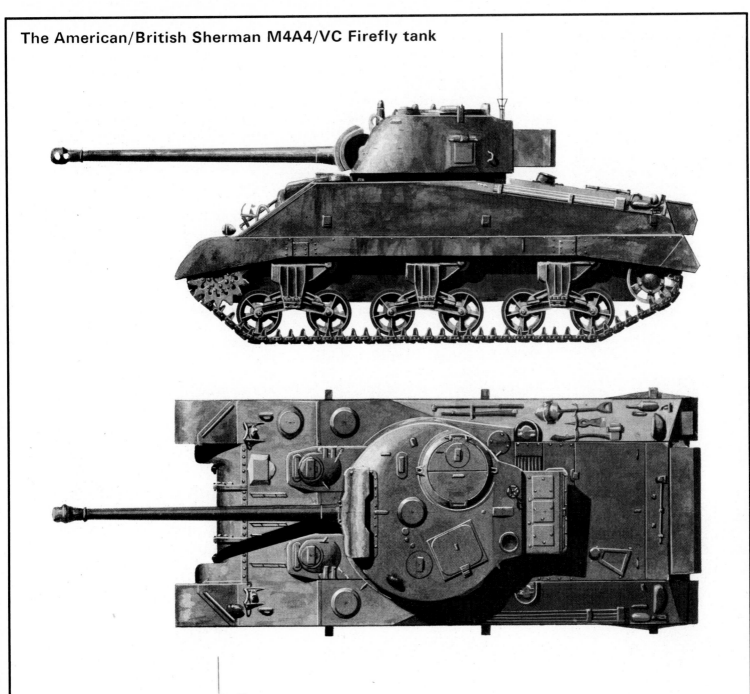

Weight: 34.8 tons.
Crew: 5.
Armament: one 76.2-mm (17-pounder) Mk. IV gun with 78 rounds, one .5-inch Browning machine gun with 500 rounds, and one .3-inch Browning machine gun with 5,000 rounds.
Armour: hull front 51-mm, sides and rear 38-mm, belly 25-mm, and decking 19-mm; turret front 76-mm, sides and rear 51-mm, and roof 25-mm.
Engine: one Chrysler A-57 inline, 430-hp.
Speed: 25 mph on roads and 10 mph cross-country.
Range: 125 miles on roads and 50 miles cross-country.
Length: 25 feet 6 inches.
Width: 9 feet 6 inches.
Height: 9 feet 4 inches.

General Joseph "Sepp" Dietrich was born in 1892 in Bavaria. He was an early member of the Nazi Party, and soon after the Nazis' rise to power became a member of the *Reichstag* and of the Prussian assembly. Later he commanded Hitler's bodyguard and helped raise certain S.S. divisions. In 1942 he was given command of a corps on the Eastern Front and thereafter served in a variety of positions as a Panzer leader. He commanded the 6th *Panzerarmee* in the Ardennes.

Hasso Freiherr von Manteuffel was born into a military family in Potsdam on January 14, 1897. Educated in the Prussian cadet corps, he served in World War I. After the war he specialised in armoured warfare. In World War II he held a number of commands in France and the East. Following the July Plot he was still regarded as politically reliable and given the command of the 5th *Panzerarmee* during the Ardennes offensive. In April 1945 he led the 3rd *Panzerarmee*.

640 Panther and Pzkw IV tanks available to Dietrich, Manteuffel's three Panzer divisions had only been restored to about two-thirds of their full strength, about 320 tanks in all. And in fact, if they had been at full strength, the fuel problem would have been even more acute than it was. According to the plan, the Panzers should have attacked with sufficient petrol for five refuellings, which would have given them a range of up to 170 miles; on the day of the attack, they had only enough for two refills, as for camouflage reasons Hitler had forbidden the creation of fuel dumps close to the line. More important, he had made no allowances either for the difficult terrain or for the very bad weather. On December 28, describing the failure of the Ardennes offensive to his generals, Hitler described as follows the misfortunes that befell the 12th *"Hitlerjugend"* Panzer Division on the roads of the Ardennes:

"Only the first wave of the 12th S.S. Panzer Division's tanks were in action, whilst behind them there was an enormous convoy jammed solid, so that they could go neither forward nor back. Finally, not even the petrol could get through. Everything was stationary, and the tanks' engines were merely idling. To avoid frost damage, etc., the engines had to be run all night, which also had the advantage of keeping the men warm. This created enormous petrol requirements. The roads were bad. They could only use first gear . . . there was no end to it."

Skorzeny's special forces

Among the special forces used during this operation, mention should be made of the so-called 150th Panzer Brigade, made up of about 2,000 men conversant with American army slang, using jeeps and even old Sherman tanks rescued from the battlefield. The brigade had a double purpose: firstly, small patrols were to infiltrate the enemy lines and cause panic by spreading alarmist rumours and sabotaging telephone communications and signposts; then, when the breakthrough was being exploited, small motorised columns would be sent out to capture the Meuse bridges and hold them until the rest of the armour arrived.

This "Trojan horse" invented by Hitler was placed under the command of Otto Skorzeny, who had been promoted to colonel after capturing Admiral Horthy. The stratagem, which was quite contrary to the Geneva Convention, had some initial success because of its surprise element, but the counter-measures immediately devised by the Americans were most effective. Germans captured in American uniforms were immediately tried and shot, although some of them had only taken part in the operation when threatened with a German firing-squad.

The paratroops who spread terror throughout Belgium, and even as far as the outskirts of Paris, never numbered more than 1,200, discounting the dummies used, and were commanded by Lieutenant-Colonel Heydte; but the pilots of the Junkers Ju 52's from which they were to jump were so badly trained that three-quarters of them jumped behind the German lines. The Allies thought they had been entrusted with the task of killing Eisenhower, but post-war research has revealed how groundless these suppositions were, although they did interfere with the normal functions of the Allied high command.

Inadequate reserves

Behind the first wave of troops, there were eight reserve divisions, seven of which were subject to O.K.W. orders. Model thus found himself with very little chance of exploiting any slight advantages he might gain without referring to Hitler. In addition there were two newly formed Panzer brigades, but that was all.

Theoretically, the attack was to be supported by 3,000 bombers and fighter-bombers, but on the first day a mere 325 planes took off, of which 80 were jets. Hitler could not bring himself to expose German towns to Allied air attacks by depriving them of fighter cover.

On December 10, O.K.W. left Berlin for Ziegenberg near Giessen, where, in preparation for the 1940 Blitzkrieg against France, a command post—never used—had been set up. It was here that two days later, having first made them hand in their pistols and brief-cases, Hitler harangued the commanders of the units engaged in this action. "There were about 30 generals including divisional commanders," writes Jacques Nobécourt. "They had been brought from Koblenz during the night by bus, twisting, turning, and going back on its tracks to deceive them regarding the

route being followed. All along the wall of the lecture hall stood S.S. men keeping an eagle eye on all present."

"No one in the audience dared move, or even take out a handkerchief," wrote Bayerlein, commander of the Panzer-*"Lehr"*, who thought Hitler looked ill and depressed.

"For two solid hours Hitler spoke, using no notes." Although we do not have the authentic verbatim account of his speech, the French version presented by Raymond Henry takes up 11 pages of his book. In it, Hitler once more reminded his listeners of the steadfastness of Frederick the Great refusing to surrender in 1761, in spite of the heavy pressure exerted on him by his brother, his ministers, and his generals; and Hitler spoke of the weakness of the coalition opposing Germany:

"On the one hand the ultra-capitalist states, on the other ultra-marxist states; on the one hand a great empire, the British Empire, slowly dying; on the other a colony just waiting to take over. Countries whose aims are becoming more and more different day by day. And if you watch closely, you can see differences arising hour by hour. A few well-struck blows and this artificial common front could come crashing down at any moment."

When Hitler had finished, Rundstedt assured him of the devoted loyalty of all his generals.

In the Allied camp

Amongst the Allies, the battle of the Ardennes was and has been the subject of considerable argument. It allowed Montgomery once more to lay claim to the title of head of Allied land forces, and even today the discussion rages between supporters of the American supreme commander and of his brilliant but independent second-in-command; just as for 20 years after the disappointing Battle of Jutland, there were divisions between supporters of Admiral Beatty, and those of Admiral Jellicoe. In his *Memoirs,* published in 1958, Montgomery expresses himself with his usual freedom, whereas Eisenhower, both during his tenure of the White House and during his later retirement, maintained a discreet silence.

We are here simply concerned with two questions: the first concerns the Allied forces holding the Ardennes, the second concerns the surprise offensive of December 16, 1944.

It must first be noted that with his right wing north of Trier and his left in the Losheim gap, south of Monschau, Major-General Middleton, commanding the American VIII Corps, held an 80-mile front with only four divisions. The 4th and 28th Divisions had been badly mauled in the unsuccessful attack on the

△ Patton on a inspection tour. Unlike most of his compatriots, Patton realised that a major offensive through the Ardennes might be coming, and had already started laying contingency plans for switching his 3rd Army's axis of advance from east to north. This would take the German offensive in flank and crush it.

Rur dams; the 9th Armoured Division (Major-General John W. Leonard) had never been under fire, nor had the 106th Division (Major-General Alan W. Jones) which had only taken over the Schnee Eifel sector of the front on December 11, after trailing all through France and southern Belgium in freezing rain and open lorries.

But did the Americans have any choice? In his *A Soldier's Story,* General Bradley explains the situation in a perfectly convincing way: to give Middleton more troops would have meant taking troops away from the two groups due to attack, to the north and south, in November. Even as it was, Hodges and Simpson had only 14 divisions between them for their 60-mile front north of the Ardennes, whilst to the south, Patton had only nine divisions, stretched over a 90-mile front. The Americans were so short of troops that the offensive was put back a week so that they could get back from Montgomery just one division they had lent him to mop up the Scheldt estuary. And to concentrate the 3rd Army's attack on a narrow front, the Americans had to transfer part of Patton's sector to Devers's 6th Army Group. If they had wanted to reduce the risks of a German attack against Middleton's thinly held Ardennes positions, the Americans could have cancelled Patton's offensive, as Montgomery had suggested, and even

dug in along the front for the winter. Both these alternatives were, to Bradley, out of the question. Middleton's forces would be stretched as thinly as possible, risking the chance of an enemy attack, and the Americans would throw all available divisions into the November offensive. Thus troops were taken away from the Ardennes to reinforce the winter offensive. It was a calculated risk which Bradley had decided to take, and one to which he stuck both during and after the event. It was not the safest solution, but if the Allies had worried more about such considerations, they would have had to winter outside the burnt-out shell of Paris.

Eisenhower, whilst claiming his due share of responsibility, justifies Bradley:

"The responsibility for maintaining only four divisions on the Ardennes front and for running the risk of a large German penetration in that area was mine. At any moment from November 1 onward I could have passed to the defensive along the whole front and made our lines absolutely secure from attack while we awaited reinforcements. My basic decision was to continue the offensive to the extreme limit of our ability, and it was this decision that was responsible for the startling successes of the first week of the German December attack."

It seems quite clear, after this, that the calculated risk about which Eisenhower

and Bradley talk was not something dreamed up after the event to excuse the weaknesses of their actions.

Hitler underestimated

It must be admitted, however, that Eisenhower and Bradley calculated things very tightly, as neither imagined for one minute that Hitler would fix Antwerp as the objective for his Panzers. And, of course, their reasoning followed the same lines as that of Model, Rundstedt, and Manteuffel, who all declared that the plan was impracticable and would have the most catastrophic consequences.

When he became aware of enemy troop concentrations, Colonel Dickson, head of General Hodges's Intelligence staff, said on December 10 that the defence of the Reich was based on the following strategy: the halting of the Allied offensive, followed by a counter-attack, with all forces concentrated between the Rur and the Erft.

In other words, Dickson assumed that if there was a counter-attack, it would follow the lines of the "little solution" that Rundstedt and Model had unsuccessfully suggested to Hitler, since more ambitious plans were far beyond the Wehrmacht's capabilities.

The Allies were thus quite aware that German troops had been brought into position in readiness for a counter-attack, but they thought that these concentrations would form a flank attack on Hodges's troops preparing to attack Cologne, and that it would be combined with the breaching of the Rur dams. Later, Dickson's assumption was taken as being the correct one, and it was only on the day before the attack took place that Allied Intelligence found out that rubber boats and other craft had been assembled on the German side of the River Our.

Oddly enough, Colonel Koch, head of the American 3rd Army's Intelligence staff, was more worried than Dickson about the American situation; he even managed to get General Patton to share his apprehension, since on December 12 the latter ordered his chief-of-staff to work out "a study of what the Third Army would do if called upon to counter-attack such a break-through". And on the night of December 15-16, when he knew that the enemy was observing radio silence, he said "I want you, gentlemen, to start making plans for pulling the Third Army out of its eastward attack, change the direction ninety degrees, moving to Luxemburg and attacking north."

With all the information before us, Bradley was probably right when he said that although the Allies may have been wrong about the enemy's intentions, their estimate of his capabilities at that time was on the whole correct. For–and events were to bear this out in the following weeks–against forces as large as the Allies', Rundstedt did not have the resources necessary to ensure the success of an offensive strategy.

Thus, because they had failed to reckon with Adolf Hitler's megalomania, the Allied chiefs were caught badly napping on December 16–not least Field-Marshal Montgomery, who on the very morning of the German offensive had summed up the enemy's possibilities of action in the following words:

"The enemy is at present fighting a defensive campaign on all fronts, his situation is such that he cannot stage major offensive operations. Furthermore, at all costs he has to prevent the war from entering on a mobile phase; he has not the transport or the petrol that would be necessary for mobile operations, nor could his tanks compete with ours in the mobile battle."

▽ *Lieutenant-General Leonard T. Gerow. As a major-general, Gerow commanded the American V Corps, which was holding the sector of the Ardennes front attacked by the right wing of Dietrich's 6th* Panzerarmee.

CHAPTER 141
Battle of the Bulge

On the first day of the offensive, the 6th S.S. *Panzerarmee* attacked with its infantry divisions, keeping its Panzers in reserve to exploit the initial success. On the right it came up against the American 2nd and 99th Divisions, of V Corps, still commanded by Major-General Leonard Gerow; the 2nd Division was an experienced, battle-hardened unit which overcame its surprise very quickly, whereas the 99th Division, which had never before seen major action, had more difficulty in recovering its composure. In the end, V Corps managed to hold on to the Elsenborn ridge in spite of all enemy attacks. But Dietrich easily broke through the Losheim gap, lightly held by the 14th Armoured Division, which opened up the road to Stavelot, and in addition enabled him to turn the left flank of the 106th Division.

On the very same day this division was pierced on its left by the 5th *Panzerarmee*'s attack, which also threw back the 28th Division towards Clervaux (Clerf). The two regiments of the 106th Division holding the Schnee Eifel plateau were in imminent danger of being surrounded.

The 7th Army, reduced to four divisions, had to be satisfied with pivoting

▽ *German infantry on the move. Instead of smashing open the American front with his Panzer divisions, Dietrich decided to open the breach with his infantry and then exploit it with his armour. The result was that the offensive never really gathered momentum.*

◁ Obersturmbannführer *Jochen Peiper (left), commander of the celebrated* Kampfgruppe *"Peiper", halts in his command car to read a signpost.*
▽ *German infantryman, laden down with ammunition, weapons, and entrenching equipment. In this last major offensive on the Western Front, the Germans used up the few remaining first-class fighting troops they still had, and from now on the burden was to fall on second rate troops and even the* Volkssturm.

around Echternach, instead of including Luxembourg in its plan of attack, as originally planned. Although it had to yield some ground, the American 4th Division, which made up Middleton's right flank, was less severely tested than the 28th.

When the first news of the German attack reached S.H.A.E.F., Bradley was in Versailles, conferring with General Bedell Smith, Eisenhower's chief-of-staff. A few hours later, a further report indicated that the American 1st Army had identified eight German divisions.

Eisenhower and Bradley immediately realised the implications of this offensive, but the forces available to them on December 16 were even less than those available to General Gamelin on May 13, 1940. They were in fact limited to XVIII Airborne Corps (Major-General Ridgeway), two of whose divisions, the 82nd and the 101st, were being reformed near Rheims, after two months' action in the Nijmegen salient. This corps was immediately alerted, and the 9th and 3rd Armies received orders to make their 7th and 10th Armoured Divisions respectively available to the 1st Army.

In a few days' time Eisenhower would also be able to call upon the 2nd Armoured Division, which had just landed in France, as well as the 87th Division and the 17th Airborne Division, which were still in England, but about to embark for France. Even then it would take time for them to come into the line, and meanwhile the Americans could put up only six divisions against 21 German.

In addition, although the successes of Skorzeny's commandos and von der Heydte's paratroopers were very slight, rumour greatly magnified them. Above all, the bad weather of that week reduced air strikes almost to nil, whereas at Mortain, on August 7, the U.S. 9th Air Force had proved itself to be "the most effective anti-tank gun in existence". But "low cloud" and "thick fog" were phrases that the weather forecasters repeated with monotonous regularity throughout the week December 16-23.

The Germans waver

In the public mind the Ardennes campaign is summed up in the one word: Bastogne, and rightly so, since Brigadier-General A. C. McAuliffe and his 101st Airborne Division fought heroically around the little town, although the behaviour under fire of the 7th Armoured Division and its commander, Brigadier-General Robert Hasbrook, was also worthy of the highest praise. Between December 18 and 22, the defensive position of Saint Vith compelled the 5th *Panzer-armee* to disperse its energies, and the town was only evacuated after an express order.

It is true that on December 19, in the Schnee Eifel plateau region, two regi-

ments of the 106th Division were trapped, and 6,000 men had to surrender, but everywhere else the Americans stood up gallantly under all the attacks. As Jacques Mordal very rightly says:

"The great merit of the American troops was that despite the surprise and initial disorder, a few commanders and a few handfuls of troops were found who saved the situation by holding on grimly to certain vital positions; and it may be said that rarely has the fate of so many divisions depended on a few isolated engagements. A mere handful of artillerymen firing their few guns saved Bütgenbach on December 16, and prevented the complete isolation of the 2nd and 99th Divisions. A battalion of sappers was to save Malmédy; and a company of the 51st Engineer Combat Battalion stopped the advance of the leading elements of *Kampfgruppe* 'Peiper'. They blew up the Trois-Ponts bridge across the Salm, and forced Peiper to go back via Amblève, and find a further bridge at Werbomont,

◁ *German troops pass a knocked-out American motor transport column.*
▽ ◁ *German soldiers help themselves to clothing and equipment from American dead. Note the bare feet of the corpse on the left.*
▽ *A Königstiger or Tiger II heavy tank advances through the heavily-forested Ardennes hills.*

where the pioneers of the 291st Battalion fought heroically to prevent his crossing; for the second time the German troops saw a bridge being blown up in front of them, and they also suffered severe losses from air attacks launched in spite of the bad weather.

"Stavelot, lost on December 17, was recaptured two days later. The battle went on in the sunken valley of the Amblève, where after five days of hard combat, Peiper, out of fuel, was forced to leave behind all his equipment and withdraw the few hundred men remaining on foot, in the snow, and following impossible tracks."

Slow advance

On the German side, Dietrich made the big mistake of stubbornly trying to take the Elsenborn ridge, whose defences had been greatly strengthened by the transfer to General Gerow of that first-class fighting unit, the American 1st Division; thus the 12th "Hitlerjugend" S.S. Panzer Division was halted around Bütgenbach. As for the celebrated "Leibstandarte", it became separated from its advanced elements, which had pushed forward into the Amblève valley, on Colonel Peiper's orders. In short, four days after the initial attack, the 6th *Panzerarmee* was still far from the Meuse bridges–which it should have reached within 72 hours.

Bastogne reached

On Dietrich's left, Manteuffel had shown more tactical flair, being further helped by the fact that General Hodges was finding it more difficult to reinforce his VIII Corps in Luxembourg than between Elsenborn and Trois-Ponts; Clervaux and Wiltz fell easily, thus opening up the way to Bastogne. Faced with this most unexpected development–for after all, it had been thought that Dietrich's forces would have the starring rôle in this offensive–Model and Rundstedt recommended the immediate transfer of II S.S. Panzer Corps from the 5th to the 6th *Panzerarmee*, following the principle that successful operations ought to be exploited in preference to the less successful.

But Hitler refused categorically to allow this transfer; no doubt because he dreaded admitting, even implicitly, the failure of Dietrich and the *Waffen*-S.S., and did not want to place one of the Nazi Party's armed units under the command of the Wehrmacht generals for whom for a long time he felt nothing but mistrust, and even hate.

Had Eisenhower known that his adversary was making this tactical mistake, he would probably have refrained from taking some of the measures which marked his intervention on December 19. But with all his reports from the front indicating that Bastogne and the 101st Airborne Division were practically surrounded, he decided that the time had come to throw all his authority into the struggle. So, at 1100 hours on December 19, he convened a meeting with Bradley and Devers, together with Patton.

Eisenhower decides on his counter-offensive

According to his memoirs, Eisenhower opened the meeting by declaring that "the present situation is to be regarded

as one of opportunity for us and not disaster. There will be only cheerful faces at this conference table."

And in fact these confident phrases represented exactly the calm coolness that Eisenhower really felt on that important day. Thus the American historian Ladislas Farago, in his biography of General Patton, which he bases upon numerous unpublished documents and eye-witness accounts, has written:

"The historic Verdun conference of 19th December 1944 was, I submit, one of the high points of Dwight D. Eisenhower's generalship in the war. He was variously described as having been pale and nervous, showing not only signs of the strain but also an intimate kind of concern, as if he worried about his personal future in the aftermath of this crisis. Actually, Ike was in top form, concise and lucid, holding the conference with iron hands to its key issue–the Allied counter-attack. It was obvious to all that he knew what he wanted and was the full master of the situation. He had in full measure that special inner strength which always filled him when he was called upon to make *absolute* decisions."

◁ The penalty of failure: men of Otto Skorzeny's special commando, caught in American uniforms, are prepared for the firing squad.
▽ ◁ American prisoners are marched off to the rear past a column of advancing German armour. Note the faces of the prisoners, deliberately rendered unrecognisable.
▽ The tide begins to turn: a Tiger tank knocked out during the bitter fighting for the small town of Stavelot.

▷ *Heavily-laden Germans double across an exposed road.*
▽ *Yet again, the qualitative inferiority of Allied armour was demonstrated during the "Battle of the Bulge".*
▷▷ *American reinforcements on the way up to the front . . .*
▽▷ *. . . and in action.*

The main decision taken was to move the six divisions of General Patton's III and XII Corps from the Saar front to the Echternach–Diekirch–Bastogne front, at the same time subordinating VIII Corps to the 3rd Army. This meant that the right flank of General Devers's army group would be extended from Bitche to Saarbrücken. Such a manoeuvre had already been discussed at 3rd Army H.Q., so that a single telephone call made from Verdun by its commander was enough to get it started. According to Farago, this order, which meant the moving of 133,178 vehicles over a total of some 1,500,000 miles, was carried out in five days. During this time, the 3rd Army's rear echelons transported 62,000 tons of supplies, the Intelligence staff distributed thousands of maps of the new sector, and the communications section put down 40,000 yards of telephone cable. And all this was achieved in snow and on roads covered with black ice. This proves that Patton may have been a swash-buckler (that very day he said to Bradley: "'Brad, this time the Kraut's stuck his head in the meatgrinder.' With a turn of his fist he added, 'And this time I've got hold of the handle.'"), but he was also a thinker, and an organiser of the highest class.

Even whilst he was conferring with his subordinate commanders at Verdun, was it Eisenhower's intention to hand over command of the northern flank to Montgomery? It is impossible to say. What we do know is that Bedell Smith informed Bradley by telephone that evening that his 1st and 9th Armies were being taken over for the time being by Montgomery. Of course, since for obvious reasons Bradley was unable to leave his Luxembourg H.Q., there was a danger that he would lose telephone contact with his 1st Army command post, which was at Spa, and later moved to Liège. Nevertheless, although he did not officially protest against this regrouping, Bradley may well have feared that Montgomery would make this "for the time being" last until the unconditional surrender of the Third Reich.

Bastogne hangs on

As Bedell Smith was speaking to Bradley, the 101st Division entered Bastogne, joining up with those elements of the 9th

△ *An American dug-in mortar emplacement. From left to right the members of the crew are Private R. W. Fierdo of Wyahoga Falls, Ohio; Staff Sergeant Adam J. Celinca of Windeor, Connecticut; and Technical Sergeant W. O. Thomas of Chicago, Illinois.*

▷ *M4 Shermans of the 40th Tank Battalion lined up outside St. Vith.*

△▷ *The ruins of St. Vith after its recapture by the U.S. 7th Armoured Division.*

▷▷ En route *from Hunnange to St. Vith: men of Company C, 23rd Armoured Battalion, 7th Armoured Division.*

and 10th Armoured Divisions defending the town. The next day, XLVII Panzer Corps, following its instructions, by-passed the town to north and south, leaving the 26th *Volksgrenadier* Division the job of laying siege to it. When the commander of this formation, Lieutenant-General Heinz Kokott, called upon General McAuliffe to surrender, he received the rudest of replies: "Nuts". The garrison's high morale was kept up, firstly, by the wholehearted support of the town population under their mayor, Monsieur Jacmin, and secondly by the sound of III Corps' guns announcing the beginning of the counter-attack in the south.

On the northern half of the bulge, an attack by the 30th Division, called by the Germans "Roosevelt's S.S.", enabled Hodges to close up the Amblève valley sector by lengthening the position held by V Corps. However, by sending in II S.S. Panzer Corps to the left of I S.S. Panzer Corps, Dietrich succeeded in re-vitalising the offensive, forcing Has-

△ △ *3rd Army infantry advance to the relief of beleaguered Bastogne.*

△ *A soldier of the 3rd Army works his way forward under a barbed wire fence about five miles from Bastogne.*

▷ *An American paratrooper, armed with a .45-inch Thompson sub-machine gun. Note the two spare magazines in his left hand.*

brook to evacuate Saint Vith on December 21. The intervention, firstly of XVIII Airborne Corps (although reduced to the 82nd Airborne Division), and secondly, of General Collins's VII Corps, comprising the 75th, 83rd, and 84th Divisions, and the 3rd Armoured Division, enabled a continuous front to be re-established on a line Manhay – Grandmenil – Hotton – Marche.

Montgomery steps in

In carrying out his tasks as commander of the 21st Army Group, Montgomery had a few difficulties with his American subordinates. His main aim was to prevent the Germans from crossing the Meuse, and provided this was done he was not very worried by the loss of a small Ardennes village here or there. He conducted the campaign according to the methods of 1918: plug the gap then, when quite ready, counter-attack. Hodges, Collins, and Ridgeway, on the other hand, hated giving up ground, and wanted to make the enemy feel the weight of their strength. To guard against every eventuality, the meticulous Montgomery established General Horrocks's British XXX Corps, comprising the 43rd, 51st, and 53rd Divisions, and the Guards Armoured Division half-way between Namur and Brussels, thereby greatly facilitating the American 1st Army's movements, which

up to December 24, had involved 248,000 men and 48,000 vehicles.

The fight goes on

By December 22, at Koblenz, Rundstedt had decided upon immediate withdrawal from the engagement, already running into trouble. Of course, Hitler, at Ziegenberg, refused to ratify this suggestion; he thought that if they threw in the O.K.W. reserves, especially the 9th Panzer and 3rd and 15th *Panzergrenadier* Divisions, they would be able to resume the offensive, or at least capture Bastogne, the main thorn in their side.

Allied air power to the fore

On December 23, an anti-cyclone brought with it a week of brilliant sunshine over the whole of the Ardennes front. The Allied air forces were immediately unleashed, flying 2,000 missions on the first day, and 15,000 in the next three days. On Christmas Eve, at a cost of 39 planes lost, 2,000 American bombers, escorted by 900 fighters, attacked the airfields near Frankfurt and the communications networks of Kaiserslautern, Bad Munster, Koblenz, Neuwied, and Euskirchen. At the same time, other air attacks were successfully launched on the enemy's

2153

rear and on certain battlefield objectives. Last, but not least, 961 Dakotas and 61 gliders were able to drop 850 tons of supplies and ammunition to beleaguered Bastogne.

On the darker side, the small town of Malmédy, already in American hands, was twice bombed in error. Whilst the 6th *Panzerarmee* was now exhausted, the 5th managed to advance yet again some 25 miles on a line Saint Hubert–Rochefort–Dinant, moving north-west.

This movement laid bare Patton's left flank, and Eisenhower transferred to the 3rd Army the 87th Division, the 11th Armoured Division, and the 17th Airborne Division. Thus, by December 24, 32 Allied divisions were in action or in reserve on the Ardennes front, against 29 German divisions calculated by S.H.A.E.F. to be involved.

△ *As the weather improved, Allied air power began to play a decisive part in the battle, not only offensively with strikes against German armour, but also defensively with supply drops. Here part of the massive Dakota fleet passes over a Sherman on its way to drop food and ammunition into Bastogne.*
▷ *Men of the U.S. 1st Army dig in on the northern side of the salient driven into the Allied front by the German attack.*
▽ *British troops, who were met by the Germans at the furthest extent of their penetration to the west. The leading Sherman is fitted with a 17-pounder gun, far superior to the more usual 75- and 76-mm guns.*

2nd Panzer Division wiped out

Faced with this further deterioration of the situation, Rundstedt renewed his plea that the offensive be abandoned. He was very strongly supported this time by General Guderian, who knew that in the East, Soviet forces were massing on the Vistula bridge-heads. Once again the Führer refused categorically, in spite of the arguments of his H.Q., only too aware of the disasters that his obstinacy would inevitably bring. In the meantime Lieutenant-General von Lauchert's 2nd Panzer Division had reached Ciney, Beauraing, and Celles, in contact with the British 29th Armoured Brigade, and only six miles from the Meuse at Dinant. On Christmas Day, it suffered a flank attack at the hands of the American 2nd Armoured Division (Major-General Harmon), which had just been transferred to VII Corps. The effect was one of total surprise, and the disaster was no less complete. By the end of the day, Lauchert's losses were as follows: 1,050 prisoners, 2,500 killed, 81 tanks (out of a total of 88), seven assault guns, all his artillery (74 pieces), and 405 vehicles. That day the American 2nd Armoured Division certainly lived up to its nickname of "Hell on Wheels". Confronted with this crushing blow, Manteuffel could only withdraw his XLVII Panzer Corps to Rochefort.

Patton relieves Bastogne

Patton's 3rd Army had a little more difficulty in relieving Bastogne, as the German 5th Parachute Division under Lieutenant-General Hellmann, on the right of the German 7th Army, put up a very spirited resistance. It was not until December 26 that the American 4th Armoured Division under Major-General Gaffey managed to link up with the beleaguered garrison, and even then it was only by means of a narrow corridor a few hundred yards wide.

Half-success into defeat

Faced with these defeats, Hitler disengaged. But was he deceiving himself, or trying to deceive others? On December 28, haranguing his generals who were about to take part in Operation *"Nordwind"*, against the American 7th Army, he pretended to be satisfied with the results of *"Herbstnebel"*:

"There is no doubt that our short offensive has had the initial result of greatly easing the situation along the whole front, although unfortunately it has not had quite the great success we expected. The enemy has been forced to abandon all idea of attack; he has been compelled to regroup his forces completely, and put back into action troops completely worn out by previous engage-

ments. His strategic intentions have been completely thwarted. The psychological factor is against him, for public opinion is bitterly critical. He now has to assert that an end to the fighting cannot be envisaged before August, perhaps before the end of the year. We have therefore a complete reversal of the situation, which was certainly not considered possible a fortnight ago."

What does all this mean? Probably that Hitler would have been far better advised to have taken his head out of the "meatgrinder", when the results were in his favour. However, instead of rapidly withdrawing his 5th and 6th *Panzerarmee* behind the *Westwall,* he insisted

△ *Private Frank Vukasin of Great Falls, Montana, reloads his Garand M1 beside the corpses of two Germans during the 83rd Division's attack towards Houffalize.*

▽ *The bitterness of the fighting for Bastogne can be gauged from this photograph of German dead caught by American machine gun fire after their protecting tanks had been knocked out.*

on their trying to hold the Ardennes salient in impossible conditions, so turning his half-success of December 16 into a clear failure. That this is so is clear from the losses of the two sides: in manpower the Americans had suffered 76,890 casualties to the Germans' 81,834; in tanks 733 to 324; and aircraft 592 to 320. Whereas the Americans could replace their *matériel* losses with little difficulty, the Germans could not.

When one realises that German possibilities of rebuilding the Wehrmacht's strength were slowly diminishing, and that on January 12, 1945 Stalin unleashed his fifth and last winter offensive, there is no doubt that these figures confirm the German defeat, not only in the Ardennes, but on the whole of the Western Front.

The abandonment of Operation *"Herbstnebel"* on December 27 (to the despair of Guderian), did not mean a reinforcement of the Eastern Front forces, for as Hitler said:

"Militarily, what is vital is that we should pass from this sterile defensive phase on to the offensive. Attack is the only means by which we can make the war in the West run in our favour." And he added: "Our task now must be the annihilation, by a series of isolated attacks, of enemy forces south of a line made by the breach in the Ardennes line. The following operation will be linked to that. I hope that we will thus be able to destroy the enemy, starting with the American units in the south. After that we will continue the attack, bringing it within the framework of the central operation."

This programme seems rather close to that which Ludendorff tried to carry out against the Allies in summer 1918, except that the Central Powers were not fighting Russia as well.

HIMMLER'S PRIVATE ARMY

Heinrich Himmler was the only top-ranking Nazi leader to come from Bavaria, where the movement had been born. He became identified in the eyes of the world as the black-uniformed figure-head of Nazi terror, arch-priest of the "Master Race", and the leading policeman of the Reich. He was *Reichsführer*-S.S.–the S.S. National Leader–but he was not the man who brought the S.S. into being. Hitler was.

It happened at the end of December 1924, when Hitler emerged from Landsberg jail, a wiser and more dangerous re-volutionary than the man who had led the original party bullies through the streets of Munich on the morning of November 9, 1923. For a start he wanted a personal bodyguard force with no duty but to himself; and he had the material ready to hand. These were the members of the *Schutz-staffeln*–the "protection squads"

–formed before the Munich *Putsch*. Completely apart from Ernst Röhm's private army, the *Sturmabteilungen* or S.A., the S.S. began as a tiny force–20 men to a city. And when Hitler held his first public rally after his release–at Weimar in July 1926–200 S.S. men took part in the march-past and received a "blood flag" for their part in the Munich *Putsch*. Three years later the S.S. had grown no larger when Hitler gave it a new commander: Heinrich Himmler.

Himmler, ex-fertiliser sales-man and chicken farmer, was a protégé of Hitler's party rival, Gregor Strasser, for whom he had worked as secretary. He got him-self the reputation of being a man with no cast-iron political views–apart from a conveniently vague devotion to National Socialism and the concepts of blood, soil, and race. Such a man would have been a natural choice

for what Hitler needed in 1929: a pliant nonentity to lead "his" S.S., for by that year Hitler was clashing with his party rivals and Röhm's S.A. In the turbulent months between 1929 and 1932, when Hitler came to terms with his rivals and pre-served the unity of the Party, the S.S. remained a static factor. It even came under Röhm's direct orders. (Large-scale recruitment dated from 1931, and by April 1932 it had risen to a strength of 30,000.) Nor was it at all instru-mental in the appointment of Hitler as Reich Chancellor in January 1933. But once Hitler was in the saddle the S.S. took on a new significance as the only force able to tackle the S.A. if it should come to a showdown.

And a showdown was what Hitler wanted. He had obtained the tacit consent of the Army and Navy commanders to a settling of accounts with the S.A. And

△ Reichsführer-*S.S. Heinrich Himmler, head of one of the most sinister and powerful private armies the world has ever seen.*
▽ *Himmler inspects men of the 14th "Galizische" S.S. Grenadier Division during June 1944. The division, a non-Germanic one, was raised from Ukrainian nationalists in 1943.*

Hitler's main instrument in the "Blood Purge" of 1934, which shattered the S.A. for ever, was the brutal efficiency of the S.S. murder squads. But by the time of the "Blood Purge" the kernel of the future *Waffen*-S.S. had already been brought into being.

This was the S.S.-*Stabswache* or "Headquarters Security Guard", raised in Berlin in March 1933. A small force of armed troopers, it was expanded and given its official title on Nazi Party Day (May Day) of the same year: "S.S.-*Leibstandarte* Adolf Hitler" (Adolf Hitler's S.S. Life Guards). *Leibstandarte* was destined to become to first regiment of the *Waffen*-S.S.–the Field S.S.

First phase in the development of the *Waffen*-S.S. was the raising of S.S.-*Verfügungstruppen* or Armed Reserve Troops throughout the Reich–drilled and armed units up to battalion strength, officially defined as "exclusively at the disposal of the Führer, for special tasks in peace and war". The strictest regulations controlled recruitment, and selection standards ("Aryan" perfection being the ideal) were almost prohibitively high. But by 1939 three S.S.-V.T. *Standarten* (regiments) had been raised: *"Deutschland"*, *"Germania"*, and *"Der Führer."* The S.S.-V.T. troops took part in the successive occupations of Austria, the Sudetenland, and Czechoslovakia and had established their niche in the German military machine.

Parallel with the S.S.-V.T. were the *Totenkopfverbände* (the "Death's Head" Detachments) of the S.S. Originally raised as concentration camp guards, the *Totenkopf* units were intended to be used in the event of any civil strife caused by Germany's going to war. In 1937 they were reconstituted into three regiments –*"Oberbayern"*, *"Brandenburg"*, and *"Thuringen"*, with a fourth (*"Ostmark"*) being added after the Austrian *Anschluss*. A typical *Totenkopf* unit raised in 1939 was *"Heimwehr Danzig"*, recruited from ethnic Germans in the Danzig area and used to police the city and its precincts. After the Polish campaign (in which the *Leibstandarte* and S.S.-V.T. regiments served), changes came thick and fast. The three S.S.-V.T. regiments were re-formed as the *"Verfügungsdivision"*. *Leibstandarte* was raised to the

◁ *Before the war: an honour guard of the "Leibstandarte". By 1939 it was a motorised division, as which it served in Poland and France. In 1942 it was converted into a Panzer division, under the command of Sepp Dietrich, and from then to the end of the war was used as a "fire brigade" division on the Western and Eastern Fronts. Originally formed as Hitler's bodyguard, the "Leibstandarte" was the premier S.S. division.*

△ *The "Leibstandarte Adolf Hitler" on parade before the war. Once the war had started, the L.A.H. exchanged its black uniforms with white leather accoutrements for the more common field-grey service uniform.*

"Adolf Hitler, leader of the Germanic peoples, I swear loyal and faithful obedience unto you, and those that you place in authority over me, unto death. So truly help me God!"

strength of a fully motorised infantry regiment. A new division was formed from the cream of the *Totenkopfverbände* – the *"Totenkopf"* Division. Yet another was raised from the police forces: the *"Polizei"* Division. In addition there were independent *Totenkopf* regiments, plus the three S.S. officers' academies (*"Braunschweig"*, *"Bad Tölz"*, and *"Graz"*), and the S.S. *Verwaltungsführerschule* – the Administration School.

Even before the 1940 offensive opened, recruiting had already begun outside the Reich. A new S.S. regiment, *"Nordland"*, was formed on the basis of Danish and Norwegian volunteers. Another, *"Westland"*, was recruited in Holland and Belgium. Later in the year they were merged with *"Germania"* Regiment to form the

"Germania" Division, and the *"Verfügungsdivision"* was re-christened *"Das Reich"*. *"Germania"* was re-christened as *"Wiking"*.

Two of the *Totenkopf* regiments (5th and 6th) were re-formed into *Kampfgruppe "Nord"*; four others were merged in pairs (8th and 10th, 4th and 14th) to create the 1st and 2nd (S.S.) Motor Brigades. At the same time two S.S. cavalry regiments (1st and 2nd) were formed from independent cavalry units, cycle units, and horse artillery elements.

The training of this new S.S. force was entrusted to Paul Hausser, an ex-regular army staff officer in World War I who joined the S.S. in November 1934. His first task was officer cadet training, but by 1939 the strict new methods applied to the entire

force. Discipline was at the very highest pitch, and standards were so high that one out of three S.S. men applying for a walking-out pass failed to measure up because of turn-out.

Despite all this spit-and-polish and hard training, the S.S. divisions did not do well in their first real baptism of fire: the 1940 campaign in the West. *"Totenkopf"* in particular earned early notoriety for its massacre of surrendered British soldiers at Le Paradis farm near Bailleul. But it was after this campaign that the term *"Waffen-S.S."* was first used in its currently-known context. And in September Himmler declared his intention to expand the force again: "We must attract all the Nordic blood of the world to us and deprive our adversaries of it."

▽ *Men of the 12th "Hitlerjugend" Panzer Division swear the oath of allegiance to the Führer.*

TOI AUSSI /
TES CAMARADES T'ATTENDENT
DANS LA DIVISION FRANÇAISE DE LA
WAFFEN·SS

Voluntee

When it came to interpreting what was really meant by "Nordic blood", Himmler's standards were, to say the least, elastic. They were made even more complicated by the decision to expand the *Waffen*-S.S. into a "New European Army". And one of the foreign units which always got good press coverage in German publications such as *Signal* and *Wehrmacht* was the diminutive force recruited from Germany's ancient enemy, France.

Gottlob Berger, Chief-of-Staff of the *Waffen*-S.S., was quoted as saying: "As a soldier I feel with the soldiers of Europe. French volunteers wear the Iron Cross next to the *Légion d'Honneur* even when they have won it in fighting Germans. Two proud decorations of the two nations on the same breast–there you have the New Europe."

But it was an embarrassing fact that the *"Charlemagne"* Division, or to give it its full title, *Waffen Grenadier Division "Charlemagne" (Französisches Nr. 1),* was not formed until the last two months of the war and was immolated in its only battle: Berlin. It was made up of survivors from the 33rd *Waffen* Cavalry Division which had been slaughtered at Budapest. To these remnants were added elements from two original French volunteer units.

The first of these was the Wehrmacht French Volunteer Infantry Regiment No. 638 and the second was the *"Légion Tricolore",* which by 1944 had been built up to brigade strength with the title of *"S.S. Freiwilligen Sturmbrigade 'Charlemagne' Nr. 6".* These men wore the tricolour shield of France on the right sleeves of their German-pattern uniforms; but no grandiose title could disguise the fact that their numbers were vestigial. It was not until 1944 that they were reinforced to regimental strength, and the *"Charlemagne"* Division itself was little more than a brigade. The holocaust of Berlin was their first battle–and their last.

◁ *Recruiting poster for the 33rd "Charlemagne" French S.S. Grenadier Division.*
▷ *Men of the 638th French Volunteer Infantry Regiment, transferred to the S.S. en bloc in August 1943.*

...and from Denmark

△ *Three Danish brothers in S.S. sports dress at a training depot in Alsace. They are members of 24th "Danmark" S.S. Panzergrenadier Regiment "Danisch Nr. 1". By the spring of 1943 several Germanic foreign S.S. contingents had been amalgamated with a cadre from the 5th "Wiking" S.S. Panzergrenadier Division (formed in 1940 from Germanic volunteers) to form the 11th "Nordland" S.S. Freiwilligen Panzergrenadier Division.*

▷ *Hauptsturmführer (Captain) Frederik von Schalburg, commander of the "Freikorps Danmark" from February 1942 to his death in action near Demy'ansk on the following June 2. In 1943, the Danish branch, or "Germansk-Korps", of the Germanische-S.S. was renamed the "Schalburg-Korps" after the man Himmler had considered one of the best examples of S.S. material he had ever seen.*

▷▷ *Danish S.S. recruiting poster.*

The recruiting of Danish volunteers into the *Waffen*-S.S. followed two main streams. It began in 1940 when the 5th S.S. *Panzergrenadier* Division *"Wiking"* was formed. This was based on the former *"Germania"* Regiment and included the first regiment of Danish volunteers. These wore the Danish S.S. emblem–a white circular swastika–on their arm shields.

Next came *"Freikorps Danmark"*, one of the many non-German volunteer legions initially trained under German N.C.O.s, but later receiving officers and N.C.O.s of their own nationality. These men could be transferred to regular *Waffen*-S.S. units; if so, they tended to retain their distinctive armshields.

In 1943 the *Waffen*-S.S. underwent a new reorganisation which involved the re-grouping of the foreign legions. *"Freikorps Danmark"* became the 24th S.S. *Panzergrenadier* Regiment *"Danmark"*. The regiment soldiered on in Russia with the new *Waffen*-S.S. Division *"Nordland"*, formed early in 1943 from predominantly Scandinavian units. Finally came the 3rd *Panzergrenadier* Regiment *"Danmark"*, which formed part of the notorious *"Totenkopf"* Division. The veterans of *"Freikorps Danmark"* and *"Nordland"* fought their last battle at Berlin in 1945.

Here it should be remembered that it was the *foreign* contingents of the *Waffen*-S.S. which did as much as anyone to establish the ferocious reputation of the force in general. Their status as combatants was unorthodox and remained undefined throughout that war. German troops of the *Waffen*-S.S., if captured, could expect to receive normal P.O.W. treatment. But foreign *Waffen*-S.S. men could end up with the death sentence as traitors. Hence their tendency–documented in many an action–to fight with fanatical tenacity. It could even be claimed that these foreign troops, few though they were in number, were the only forces on which Hitler could rely in full by the last weeks of the war.

FOR DANMARK!
MOD BOLCHEVISMEN!

2165

△ *Highly competitive sporting events were run at S.S. training depots to improve basic physical fitness, build up an* esprit de corps, *and develop teamwork.*

△▷ *A 17-year old volunteer Norwegian gunner of the S.S. (by the wheel). Note the camouflage smock and helmet cover, worn from the early days of the war by S.S. troops.*

△▷▷ *Two Flemish S.S. volunteers at work clearing a stoppage in their MG 34 machine gun. They too are wearing camouflage smocks and helmet covers and are probably members of the "Westland" S.S. Infantry Regiment, which was incorporated into the "Wiking" Division, the best foreign division in the S.S., in December 1940.*

▷△ *The lighter side? An S.S. volunteer whiles away his spare time painting.*

▷▽ *A Dutch volunteer, lately a clerk, learns a more exacting trade: that of the sniper.*

▷▷ *A lesson in tactical reconnaissance at a training depot. The Waffen-S.S. were noted for the ruthlessness and aggression of their fighting more than for the finer points of the military art.*

▷▷▷ *S.S. assault pioneers train at boatwork.*

◁ ◁ *An S.S. recruiting poster for Norway, seeking to drum up an identity between the martial Vikings and the latter-day S.S. trooper.*
◁ *Men of the "Germanske S.S. Norge" disembark in Germany. Members of the Norwegian S.S., they had volunteered to fight on the Eastern Front and joined the "Norge" S.S. Panzergrenadier Regiment on March 11, 1943, soon afterwards forming a national company within the regiment. Norway did not prove a particularly useful recruiting area for the S.S., membership standing at only 1,247 on September 30, 1944.*

▽ A Norwegian S.S. trooper on the Eastern Front with his MG 34 machine gun. Commander of the Norwegian company on the Eastern Front was Obersturmführer (1st Lieutenant) Olaf Lindvig.

Norway's contribution

Norway was the only one of Germany's neutral neighbours to produce a would-be puppet ruler before being attacked, in the form of Vidkun Quisling; and there was a tendency for Himmler and Heydrich to expect great things of Norway once it had been occupied. They were soon to find out how totally mistaken Quisling had been about the national mood of the country. But—as with Denmark—they did get a hard core of S.S. volunteers.

The first Norwegian (and Danish) volunteers formed the *"Nordland"* S.S. *Panzergrenadier* Regiment, subsequently incorporated into the *"Wiking"* Division. They wore the *"Nordland"* cuff band and an arm shield bearing the Norwegian flag. Himmler's high hopes for Norway as a source of manpower were reflected in the name of the division; and argument still rages among the uniform experts of World War II over whether or not the unit wore a collar patch with the prow of a Viking ship on it.

Apart from these, there was a specialised unit of ski troops made up from Norwegian volun-teers. This was the Norwegian Ski *Jäger* Battalion *"Norge"*. It served with the 11th and 12th S.S. Mountain Rifle Regiments (*"Reinhard Heydrich"* and *"Michael Gassmair"*) in the 6th S.S. Mountain Division *"Nord"*, which was stationed on the Finnish front. Later it was transferred south to the Ardennes.

The *"Norwegen"* Foreign Legion was raised at the same time as *"Freikorps Danmark"*, after the Scandinavian campaign of April-May 1940. They followed the style of the other foreign contingents, with Army-pattern tunics and Legion arm shields. With the reorganisation of the *Waffen*-S.S. in early 1943, *"Norwegen"* became the 23rd *Panzergrenadier* Regiment *"Norge"*, grouped with its opposite number, 24th *Panzergrenadier* Regiment *"Danmark"*, to form the *Panzergrenadier* Division *"Nordland"*, serving in Russia and then Berlin.

With the Norwegian S.S. it was basically the same story: nominal divisions way under strength. Altogether, about 6,000 Danes and Norwegians served in the ranks of the *Waffen*-S.S.

ons antwoord:
Het geweer
ter hand!

Grijpland
Nijpland
Engeland

Vlamingen
alle in de ϟϟ Langemarck!

The Dutch SS

Together with the Danes and Norwegians, the Dutch were officially regarded as "super-*Untermensch*" in Himmler's crackpot hierarchy of racial superiority. Certainly they produced a champion crop of volunteers for the *Waffen*-S.S. which has been put as high as 50,000. In Holland the Germans were able to call on the pro-Fascist adherents of Mussert; in Belgium there were the Flemish and Walloon followers of Léon Degrelle, who became a field commander as well as a quisling leader.

Recruiting from the Low Countries began with the Volunteer Regiment *"Nordwest"*, including both Dutch and Belgian nationals. In addition there were the Belgian and Dutch Foreign Legions, *"Flandern"* and *"Niederlande"*. For the Dutch, the evolution from foreign legion to S.S. *Panzergrenadier* regiment

produced the 23rd *Freiwilligen Panzergrenadier* Division *"Nederland"*, formed round two regiments: the 48th Volunteer *Panzergrenadier* (*"General Seyffart"*) and the 49th (*"De Ruyter"*). It had to wait until December 1944 before receiving official divisional status, and it was typical of the tangled story of the *Waffen*-S.S. that it only got its number – 23 – when another 23 (*"Kama"*) was disbanded. The *"Nederland"* Division served with Army Group *"North"* on the Leningrad/Kurland front. Trapped in Kurland by the Russian advance, its survivors were evacuated by sea; they fought in the Stettin area, and a few were lucky enough to escape to the American lines.

The original Belgian foreign legion was the Legion *"Wallonie"*. It was up-graded to divisional status as the 28th *Freiwilligen*

Panzergrenadier Division *"Wallonie"* and suffered murderous losses on the Eastern Front under the command of Léon Degrelle. It was wiped out in the massive Oder battle of 1945, trying to halt the Russian drive on Berlin.

The second *Waffen*-S.S. formation recruited from Belgian nationals was a paper tiger. This was the 27th S.S. *Freiwilligen Panzergrenadier* Division *"Langemarck"*, which began as the 2nd S.S. Infantry Regiment (of the same name) attached to the *"Das Reich"* Division in Russia in 1942. The following year it was up-graded to brigade status under the title *"Langemarck Sturmbrigade"*. *"Langemarck"* ended the war as a nominal division; but it never exceeded its basic brigade strength and, like its stable-mate *"Wallonie"*, was ground to pieces on the Eastern Front.

NEDERLANDERS

VOOR UW EER EN GEWETEN OP ! - TEGEN HET BOLSJEWISME DE WAFFEN ⚡⚡ ROEPT U !

△ ◁ *A Flemish S.S. recruiting poster. From early in the war there had been a Flemish volunteer legion serving with the Germans, and in May 1943 this was expanded into a brigade under the title of the 6th "Langemarck" Freiwilligen Sturmbrigade. As such it was heavily engaged in the Ukraine and around Zhitomir between December 1943 and April 1944, when it was pulled out of the line for rest in Czechoslovakia. In July it was sent to Narva, where it was badly cut about. The brigade was again relieved in September and sent back to the depot at Hammerstein. On the 18th of the same month Himmler authorised the formation of a Flemish division, and the remnants of the "Langemarck" Brigade were amalgamated with other Flemish units to form the 27th "Langemarck" S.S. Freiwilligen Grenadier Division. The division was virtually wiped out in the last desperate battles for Germany.*

◁ *A Dutch recruiting poster for the Waffen-S.S. When the 11th "Nordland" Division was raised from northern European volunteers early in 1943, the Dutch asked for permission to raise their own national unit. The result was the 4th "Nederland" S.S. Freiwilligen Panzergrenadier Brigade, an expansion of the earlier Freiwilligen Legion "Niederlande". By autumn the brigade was 5,500 men strong and was sent to Croatia on anti-partisan operations. From there it was sent to the Leningrad front early in 1944, and then fought its way back to Lithuania, which it reached in January 1945 after suffering very heavy losses. After a rest in Danzig, the brigade was redesignated the 23rd "Nederland" S.S. Freiwilligen Panzergrenadier Division, and was wiped out in the fighting around Berlin in May.*

◁ ◁ *Opperstormleider (1st Lieutenant) J. L. Jansonius, the Dutch S.S. chief-of-staff, with a German S.S. officer (left), at a sports event at the S.S. school at Avegoor in August 1942.*

2171

from the Steppes of Russia

One of the most stupid things the Germans did in their attempt to conquer Soviet Russia was to alienate the vast majority of the population by their brutality. A careful policy of "divide and rule" with the national minorities in the Soviet Union would not only have eased the problem of diverting troops to hold down occupied territory, but would certainly have added vastly to the manpower of the Wehrmacht and its co-belligerents on the Eastern Front. As it was, it took nearly two years of fighting in Russia before it was decided to recruit troops there. Nevertheless, some of the results were impressive–on paper.

The Baltic states–only recently occupied by the Red Army when Germany invaded the Soviet Union–were naturally the first to respond. By March 1943, 22,000 Latvians and Estonians had volunteered for service. They were formed into S.S. Volunteer Brigades and were subsequently raised to the status of *Waffen Grenadier Divisionen* (19th for the Latvians and 20th for the Estonians). Tough and ferocious fighters, they were cut off in the Kurland pocket in 1945. The last Baltic S.S. unit to see action in World War II had a different story. This was the 15th *Waffen Grenadier* S.S. Division (1st Latvian), recruited from Latvian security police in 1943. Those who escaped the vicious fighting in the Baltic states and Pomerania were flung into the rag-bag garrison of Berlin, where they fought to the death.

Despite the cruelty of the German occupation, some 100,000 Ukrainians volunteered. A Russian division – the 14th *"Galizien"* – was formed, but its history was short and sharp. The division was completely wiped out in the battle of the Brody-Tarnov pocket in June 1944 (its first major engagement).

Then there were the attempts to exploit nationalist sectarian groups in Yugoslavia, raising anti-Serb forces to fight against Tito's partisans. This produced the *"Handschar"* Division: the 13th *Waffen Gebirgsdivision der S.S.* This was a force of Croatian volunteers, raised in 1943 and originally entitled *"Bosnien-Herzegowina"*. A Moslem unit, its men wore the fez, complete with silver skull-and-crossbones and eagle. During its training in France, it mutinied. When put to work in Yugoslavia it did little damage to Tito's partisans but showed itself adept in dealing out enthusiastic brutality to Yugoslav civilians. It was eventually disbanded and re-formed as a mountain regiment, retaining the same name.

Even less effective were the Albanian S.S. volunteers, from whom the 21st *Waffen Gebirgsdivision "Skanderbeg"* was formed in 1944. Its chief problem was desertion, which finally necessitated its disbandment. The same held true for the short-lived *"Kama"*, a force of Croatians.

Also raised in Russia were the 29th and 30th *Waffen Grenadier* Divisions (1st and 2nd Russian). The 29th barely saw the light of day; its personnel were almost immediately dispersed to the Russian unit being formed by the renegade General Vlassov: The R.O.A. or *Russkaya Osvoboditelnaya Armiya* ("Russian Army of Liberation"). The 30th inherited some of the former personnel of the 29th, plus *"Schumabataillone"* men – renegade Russian P.O.W.s raised by the S.S. and employed in field security duties. It was cut to pieces during the German retreat in France.

Numerous Cossack cavalry units were also raised, and although not of any importance, they were encountered frequently by the Allies during the last months of the war.

◁ *Caucasian Cossack volunteer cavalry in 1942. Later, when the rigid ethnic qualifications for the S.S. were dropped as a result of the increasingly heavy losses suffered in the East, such units were transferred to the S.S.*
▽ *Don Cossack cavalry take a rest in Russia.*

▽ Men of the 3rd "Totenkopf"
S.S. Panzer Division during a
lull in the fighting for
Smolensk in September 1941.

▷ *Men of I "Leibstandarte" S.S. Panzer Corps wait for Stukas to reduce a Russian strongpoint near Khar'kov in March 1943 before putting in the final assault. The corps was composed of three crack S.S. divisions— 1st "Leibstandarte", 2nd "Das Reich", and 3rd "Totenkopf".*

▷ ▷ *Men of an S.S. police unit ride an electric train up into the mountains of Slovenia on an anti-partisan operation in February 1944. Not members of the Waffen-S.S., the men wear Gebirgsjäger uniforms with police insignia.*

▷ ▷ ▷ *A Scandinavian volunteer of the 5th "Wiking" S.S. Division in action on the Russian Front in 1943.*

▽ Sturmbannführer *(Major)* Meyerdress (right), *holder of the Oak Leaves to the Knight's Cross of the Iron Cross, inspects a German defensive position in Russia. Meyerdress is wearing the black Panzer uniform.*

▽ ▷ *An anti-partisan patrol of S.S. mountain troops in Serbia during 1942. The men are probably from the 7th "Prinz Eugen" S.S. Gebirgsdivision.*

▽ ▷ ▷ *The commander of a "Totenkopf" Panzer unit gives his final instructions for an attack.*

Herrenvolk

....and their victims

◁ Men of the "Leibstandarte". Top row, left to right: Schütze (private), Sturmann (lance-corporal), and Rottenführer (corporal); bottom row: Unterscharführer (senior corporal), Oberscharführer (colour sergeant), and Hauptscharführer (sergeant-major).

▽ The bodies of some of the inhabitants of the village of Oradour-sur-Glane, near Limoges. On June 10, as a part of "Das Reich" Panzer Division was moving up towards Normandy, the villagers of Oradour, some 652 in all, were herded into the square and told that explosives had been reported in the village. The men were locked in barns and the women and children in the church, after which the Germans fired the village. As the men tried to flee they were machine gunned. The church was then burned down and those inside machine gunned. It was later established that 245 women, 207 children, and 190 men had been killed. Twenty S.S. men were condemned to death for the massacre after the war, and two were hanged.

◁ Another victim.

△ ◁ Troopers of the Legion
"Wallonie", a unit of Belgian
volunteers.
◁ A 7.5-cm PaK 40 anti-tank
gun of an S.S. division.
△ △ Men of an S.S. mountain
unit watch as an armoured
column passes by in February
1945.
△ S.S. troops with a rubber
assault boat in Finnish
Karelia.
▷ S.S. troopers move out from
their trench to support an
armoured assault.
△ ▷ ▷ S.S. tank riders, a
tactic copied from the
Russians.
△ ▷ Men of the Legion
"Wallonie" return from the
front.
▷ ▷ Terek Cossacks of the S.S.

OUR FLAG
IS GOING FORWARD TOO

It is only suitable that a study of the *Waffen*-S.S. and its "foreign legions" should end with one of the most ludicrous stories of the war: the attempt to form a British S.S. unit from P.O.W.s. It was a case not of a military rarity but of pure propaganda getting the upper hand. In the Nazi "Towards a New Europe" posters, the flags of all nations who had contributed as much as an under-strength renegade regiment to the *Waffen*-S.S. had been included. But the attempt to add the Union Jack to their numbers, while appearing impressive, was a particularly hopeless failure.

The fact is that the *"Britisches Freikorps"* (also known as the "Legion of St. George") never attracted sufficient recruits to make up two platoons (including officers). All the appropriate *Waffen*-S.S. heraldry had been worked out; the collar patch was to portray the three lions of England, while the cuff-band was to read *Britisches Freikorps*. But from the records, which (on both sides) are understandably thin in the extreme, the recruiting drive for the *Waffen*-S.S. attracted a total of only about 60 men by the end of the war.

The men requested that their C.O. should be an officer of right wing reputation, Brigadier Parrington, who had been captured in Greece. But this officer refused to oblige either the Germans or the Legion of St. George.

At the end of the war the unit disappeared with the collapse of the Third Reich, but there exists a rare photograph showing some of them in German uniform on the Oder front outside Berlin, serving in the S.S.-*Panzer-Aufklärungsabteilung* 11 of the S.S. *Panzergrenadier* Division *"Nordland"*.

When the division was ordered to Berlin, the small contingent was sent westwards to Templin on April 15, 1945, and here the 20 men and their sergeant disappear from the unit's records.

In perhaps the most bizarre contradiction of the S.S. racial code, the *Waffen*-S.S. accepted into its ranks near the end of the war three battalions of the "Indian National Army", under the leadership of Subhas Chandra Bose. This unit was composed of Indian Army P.O.W.s, captured in North Africa and Italy.

◁ *A poster designed to boost recruitment for the* "Britische Freikorps" *or "Legion of St. George".*

Naturally enough, by the end of the war in Europe, tactics and weapons had altered considerably in the light of the previous five years of combat experience. In the following pages we take a look at some of the land weapons that played an important part in the final operations in Europe, marked the culmination of wartime trends, or opened the way for future developments.

In the field of armour, there was a considerable increase in gunpower and protection, with increasing emphasis placed on improved suspension and scope for considerable development of the basic design. There was also a considerable proliferation in the number of self-propelled guns, particularly in the anti-tank rôle.

And with the increase in the power and protection of the tank there arose the need for weapons to cancel them out. Thus were borne the family of anti-tank missiles that have become more and more important since the end of the war.

Of course ground captured by any means had to be held by the infantry in the long run, and so the importance of their guns cannot be overemphasised. In the next few pages a few are illustrated and described.

Naturally, the weapons dealt with here are only a few of the multitude produced by governmental arms departments or improvised in the field. The list is not intended to be comprehensive, but to give an idea of the weapons in use or under development in the last months of the war.

▽ *The Russian "Katyusha".*

THE LAND WAR

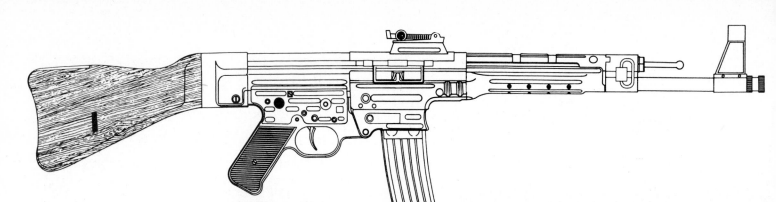

The St.G. (Sturmgewehr) 44 7.92-mm Assault Rifle. The St.G. 44 was adopted after 1944 to replace the rifle, sub-machine gun, and light machine gun of the infantry squad. It *was* a selective fire weapon with a 30 round magazine, and a cyclic rate of 500 rounds per minute. The chief feature of interest was the ammunition, 7.92-mm *kurz* or short round, which was two-thirds the weight of the standard 7.92-mm round, but at 2,300 feet per second was effective up to 400 yards. Its power and weight allowed the Germans to develop a range of assault rifles. The St.G. 44 was produced by Haenel, Mauser, and Erma, with about seven sub-contractors making the components. By February 1944, production had risen to about 5,000 a month. It weighed 11.5 lbs and had an overall length of 37 inches.

The Gewehr 43 (G43) Semi-automatic Rifle. With a ten round magazine and a weight of 9.5 lbs, the G43 or K43 was an efficient weapon. It was made from a number of stampings, castings, and forgings, and machined only where this was necessary. All G43's had a fitting to take the $1\frac{1}{2}$ power ZF 41 scope. Issued in large numbers, they were used by snipers and were even employed by the Czech Army after the war. It was 44 inches long and had a muzzle velocity of 2,550 feet per second. Variants of this weapon had a handguard of wood or plastic, and on some the bolt carrier latch, which locked the bolt and carrier to the rear, could be either on the left or the right.

The Winchester Model 1897 Trench Gun. Derived from slide-action Model 1897 shot gun, the Trench Gun has been used by the U.S. Army in almost all the wars in which it has been involved in the 20th Century, up to the Vietnam War. It was a 12-bore gun which took six cartridges loaded with nine .34 calibre shot, and was designed to take the 1917 Enfield bayonet. Though not regarded as an official weapon, it was a very effective man-stopper and was favoured for jungle operations. The Americans favoured the slide-action shot gun, which they regarded as a safer weapon than the automatic shot gun. It had an effective range of about 80 yards, but in raids and patrols would be used at much shorter ranges.

The Browning .50-inch M2 Heavy Machine Gun. The U.S. Army was one of the few armies to retain an interest in heavy calibre machine guns after World War I. The M2 weighed 81 lbs and had a 36 or 45-inch air-cooled barrel, with a cyclic rate of 400 to 500 rounds per minute. It had a muzzle velocity of 2,930 f.p.s. and a maximum range of 7,200 yards. The "50 cal" as it was known, was used as an anti-aircraft gun, both on the ground and in the air. As a ground weapon it had an awesome reputation for powerful defensive fire. It was fitted to armoured and soft skinned vehicles, and as the "quad 50" used in a four barrelled anti-aircraft mounting.

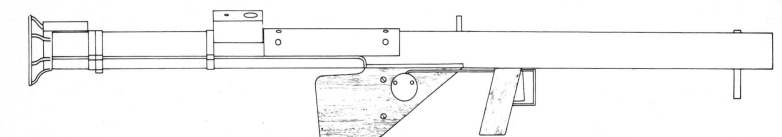

The 2.36-inch Anti-Tank Rocket Launcher. Known to the Allies as the "bazooka" after the bizarre gas-pipe horn of Bob Burns, this weapon was sighted from 100 to 400 yards. It weighed about 12 pounds and was 54 inches long. Breach-loaded, it fired a rocket by an electrical impulse from a dry cell battery fitted to the barrel. The three and a half pound rocket was capable of penetrating most armour, and a variety of warheads allowed the weapon to be used in an anti-personnel rôle. The armour-piercing properties of the rocket were the result of the "Munroe effect" of its hollow-charge warhead.

The Projector Infantry Anti-Tank. Known to the British as the "P.I.A.T.", this primitive-looking weapon could penetrate four inches of armour at short ranges. It fired a 3-lb rocket projectile, but was far from recoilless—indeed the regulation position for the operator was a prone position. One man fired the P.I.A.T. from a standing position and knocked out a Panther, but he was knocked flat by the recoil. It was parachuted to the Polish Home Army during the Warsaw Rising, and used for tank hunting by the paratroops at Arnhem. Like all infantry anti-tank weapons it required the nerves of a big game hunter to get the best results.

The 8.8-cm Raketenpanzer-büchse 54/1. At 21 lbs, this was both a heavier and a bulkier weapon than the bazooka. It was four feet four and a half inches long. The sights were designed to adjust to the different types of ammunition issued for extreme temperatures. The rockets could penetrate up to eight and a half inches of vertical armour and six inches sloped at 40°. Later marks of the *Raketen-panzerbüchse Grenate* had a range of up to 220 yards, but the propellent charge, which burned for about seven feet of the rocket's travel, necessitated the fitting of a protective shield, and made camouflage difficult. It was super-seded by the *Panzerfaust*.

The DShk 12.7-mm M1938/46 Heavy Machine Gun. Like the Browning, the DShK M1938/46 was employed as an anti-aircraft and ground weapon. It was fitted to armoured vehicles in the latter part of the war, and mounted on a small wheeled trailer. It was 62.5 inches long, weighed 78.5 lbs, and had a cyclic rate of fire of 540 to 600 r.p.m. A simple, sturdy weapon, it was air cooled, and had a relatively easily changed barrel. It is still in service with satellite armies of the Soviet Union, and has seen action in Vietnam and the Middle East. A gas-operated weapon, it uses a 50-round metallic link belt, and has a muzzle velocity of 2,822 f.p.s. On armoured vehicles it is fitted with a telescopic sight.

Tiger II (Ausf. B) "König-stiger". The Tiger II first saw action on the Russian front in May 1944, and was later employed in the Normandy area in August of the same year. It was in effect a Tiger I, but redesigned with thicker armour, sloped like that of the Panther or T-34. It mounted an 8.8-cm KwK 43 L/71 gun, two MG 34's in hull and turret, and an MG 42 on the cupola for A.A. defence. Its armour came as a shock to the Allies: the turret front, sloped at 10°, was 185-mm thick, with a superstructure front of 150-mm at 50°. The thinnest armour was 25-mm, on the hull belly. However, for this armour thickness the tank sacrificed speed: on roads it had a maximum of 25.7 m.p.h. and cross-country between 9 and 12 m.p.h. But since most German armour was used defensively in the latter part of the war, the gun and armour were more important. The Tiger II carried 80 rounds of 8.8-cm ammunition, and 5,850 rounds of machine gun ammunition. The 8.8-cm KwK 43 L/71 was the largest calibre and calibre/length gun to be employed operationally in World War II, being almost 21 feet long.

The Heavy M26 90-mm Gun Tank, Pershing. The Pershing was the result of lengthy research and development in the United States. Its gun was incorporated after the shortcomings of the 76-mm gun in the M4 had become fatally obvious in Normandy. Its 500 brake horsepower Ford Model GAF 60° V-8 inline engine gave it a maximum governed speed of 30 m.p.h. Armour varied from the upper hull front and turret front of 101.6-mm to 50.8-mm on the hull and turret rear. Auxiliary armament was two .30-inch Brownings plus another, of .50-inch calibre, on a pintle mounting on the turret. The tank carried 70 rounds of 90-mm ammunition, 500 of .30- and 550 of .50-inch. The first Pershings were assigned to the 3rd and 9th Armoured Divisions of the 1st Army. Training was conducted by a team of civilian and military instructors sent over from the United States. On V.E. Day there were 310 Pershings in Europe; 200 had been issued to the troops and 20 had seen action. Some of these were with the 9th Armoured Division when one of its units captured the Ludendorff Bridge at Remagen.

The Jagdpanzer 38(t) "Hetzer". Based on a widened version of chassis of the Czech TNHP-S light tank, the *Hetzer* was compact, simple, and reliable. It continued in service with the Swiss and Czech armies after World War II. It carried a 7.5-cm L/48 anti-tank gun, with a remotely controlled machine gun mounted on the roof for close defence. The six-cylinder water-cooled engine was uprated to 160 h.p. at 2,800 r.p.m. and the tracks were strengthened. Fuel capacity was increased from 48 to 73 gallons. *Hetzers* were first employed in the East, and later in the West, notably in the Ardennes offensive. A total of 1,577 vehicles was built, manufacture beginning in December 1943 at BMM and Skoda of Königgrätz.

It carried a crew of four, with 41 rounds of 7.5-cm and 600 rounds of 7.9-mm MG 34 ammunition. It had a speed of 24 m.p.h. on roads and 10 m.p.h. cross-country, with a cross-country radius of action of 60 miles. It was a typical example of a war-time conversion, attempting to provide mobile protection against massed Russian armour.

8.8-cm PaK 43/3 Panzerjäger "Jagdpanther" Sd.Kfz. 173. This was one of the most successful German tank destroyers: earlier models had proved to be either underarmoured or too slow. The *Jagdpanther* was fast, well-armoured, and mounted the deadly 8.8-cm gun. Introduced in January 1944, it had a weight of 51.3 tons, a crew of five, and a speed of 29 m.p.h. on roads and 16 to 19 cross-country. A 7.92-mm machine gun was fitted in the bow. Ammunition stowage was 60 rounds of 8.8-cm ammunition and 300 rounds of 7.9-mm ammunition. The HL 230 P30 Maybach engine developed 700 HP at 3,000 r.p.m. The *Jagdpanther* had a range of 124 miles on roads and 62 miles cross-country. With a gun range 9,000 yards and a height of 8.9 feet, the *Jagdpanther* was a formidable defensive weapon. The crew consisted of a commander, gunner, 1 or 2 loaders, wireless operator/machine gunner, and driver. By May 1945, 382 had been completed and it was intended to produce 150 vehicles a month, as the basis of the tank destroyer units in Germany's rearmed Panzer divisions.

2191

The Tank Infantry, Black Prince (A43). The Black Prince was based on the Churchill, but carried the more powerful 17-pounder gun. It was heavier than the Churchill and had a wider turret to take the bigger gun. Consequently the suspension had to be strengthened. Wider tracks, measuring 24 inches, were fitted. Six prototypes were built by Vauxhall Motors Ltd., and completed by 1945. Though the tank was never employed operationaly, it represents the culmination of the pre-war concept of the Infantry Tank. In 1946, however, in company with the early Centurion, it compared favourably with a Panther tank reconstructed by the British. The Black Prince weighed 50 tons, had a crew of five, and mounted a 17-pounder and two Besa machine guns. Armour was similar to that of the Churchill, ranging between 152-mm and 25-mm, but it had the unsatisfactory speed of 11 m.p.h. It had the Bedford Twin Six engine and Merritt Brown gearbox; and communications were provided by the No. 19 wireless set. An interesting innovation was an all-round vision cupola for the tank commander.

The Tank, Cruiser, Centaur (A27(L)). The Centaur was one example of the return to the Christie-type suspension which had proved so efficient on the Eastern Front. The Centaur IV was employed by the Royal Marine Armoured Support Group in Normandy in 1944. The earlier marks carried an auxiliary fuel tank, and mounted two Besa machine guns and a 6-pounder. Powered by a Nuffield Liberty 395 b.h.p. engine, it weighed 27.5 tons. The Cromwell I was never used in action, but a version modified as an Observation Post tank was used by some units of the Royal Artillery in North-West Europe. It was 20 feet 10 inches long, 9 feet 6 inches wide, and 8 feet 2 inches high, with a crew of five. It had a range of 165 miles. Centaurs were modified as A.A. tanks and armoured bulldozers. Centaur Mk. IV's operated by the Royal Marines mounted a 95-mm howitzer, and though intended to provide support from offshore landing craft, they were landed and gave support in the Normandy beach-head.

The Joseph Stalin 2 heavy tank. The JS-2 appeared in 1944, and mounting a 122-mm gun, it was the most powerfully armed tank in the world at that time. The chassis was based on the Klimenti Voroshilov series. The nose plate was 127-mm thick at 30°, the rolled hull sides were 89-mm thick, and the front pannier sides 133-mm thick at 12°. The driver was in the unhappy position of having no roof hatch, and had to escape either through the turret or a belly hatch well to his rear. To add to his discomfort, he had fuel tanks located either side of his seat. He fired a rigidly mounted 7.62-mm machine gun through an aperture in the glacis plate. The tank had a top speed of 27 m.p.h. and a weight of 45.5 tons, but its track width of 25.5 inches still gave it greater manoeuvrability over soft ground than the Tiger. The turret crew consisted of a commander, gunner, and loader, above whom was a hatch which incorporated a mounting for a 12.7-mm DShK anti-aircraft machine gun. The turret was cramped, dominated by the 122-mm gun, with a low roof, and a turret ring restricted by the hull sides.

The JSU-152 assault gun. This is another example of the Klimenti Voroshilov tank chassis being used to take a powerful gun. Its 152-mm M1937/43 gun could provide fast, accurate, and heavy H.E. support for advancing infantry quicker than any towed pieces. The gun had a total arc of traverse of 10° and an elevation of up to 31°; 20 rounds of A.P. and H.E. were carried, and the vehicle was fitted with a telescopic sight for direct fire. Like most Soviet A.F.V.'s it carried a 12.7-mm anti-aircraft M.G. Though it had a weight of 50 tons, this was spread on its broad tracks, and it was capable of 23 m.p.h. on roads and 10 m.p.h. cross-country. Equipped with additional tanks it had a range of 190 miles. The crew varied between four and five men. Its armour ranged from a massive 127-mm glacis plate to 19-mm on the belly, and since the vehicle stood about eight feet high, it was a formidable target for any German anti-tank gunner unfortunate enough to be in its path. The JSU-152 is still in service with the armies of the United Arab Republic and of Algeria.

The 21-cm Nebelwerfer 42.
This five-barrelled launcher
fired the 21-cm *Wurfgrenate 42
Spreng,* a rocket projectile with
a 90-pound warhead containing
22.4 lbs of T.N.T. This had a
range of 8,530 yards, though
some rockets were reported to
reach a range of 10,000 yards.
The carriage for the launcher
was derived from that for the
3.7-cm anti-tank gun. It had an
elevation from –5° to +45° and a
traverse of 12° either side. It
weighed 12 cwt and so was an
easily manoeuvred weapon.
To load, the rocket was slipped
in from the rear until a spring-
loaded clip held it secure. The
firing was done by remote control
with a hand generator. The firer
retired to cover about ten yards
from the projector. The Allies
first experienced the *Nebelwerfer*
41 in North Africa, where it was
dubbed the "Moaning Minnie"
or "Screaming Mimi" as a result
of the shriek of its missiles in
flight. Though not an accurate
weapon, it had a fast rate of fire
and high blast effect. It was
easy to manufacture and considerably cheaper than a conventional artillery piece.

The 15-cm Panzerwerfer. This
was an attempt to give the 15-cm
Nebelwerfer battlefield mobility.
The smoke trails which followed
the rockets when they had been
fired meant that the batteries had
to move from their site before
they were located and taken
under counter-battery fire. The
chassis was a 2-ton semi-track
truck, the Opel *"Maultier".*
It was lightly armoured, sufficient
to withstand small arms fire.
About 300 of these trucks, with
their Carden-Lloyd type tracks,
were produced to serve as
weapons carriers, mounting ten
15-cm barrels. In addition to the
ten rockets loaded, another ten
were carried internally. It had a
good cross-country performance,
with its 3.6-litre six-cylinder
engine giving a speed of 25 m.p.h.
over flat ground. Later it was
superseded by the more heavily
armoured Büssing-N.A.G.S.W.S.,
which came into action in 1944,
and had a greater internal stowage capacity. The drill for operating the *Nebelwerfer* was to
fire from inside the cab, and then
move off to reload the barrels.

The 7.5-cm leichtes Geschütz 40 recoilless gun. This compact and efficient weapon was first encountered by the Allies in North Africa. It was built out of an aluminium alloy which gave it a weight in action of 321 lbs. It was a mere 45.28-inches long. In action the wheels were removed. It fired an H.E. shell weighing 12-lbs 9-ozs, which had a maximum range of 8,900 yards, Armour Piercing Cored Ballistic Capped rounds weighing 15-lbs, and a 10-lb 2-oz hollow-charge shell which could penetrate 50-mm at an angle of 30° at a maximum range of 7,437 yards. In practice firing the crew observed a danger area of 110 yards to the rear of the weapon, but in action this was reduced to 55 yards. However, the blast could pick up stones and debris and the crew was advised to avoid this area. The blast could also damage ear drums and crew were warned that they should plug their ears with clay or mud. The gun was also designed so that it could not be traversed at high angles or elevated when used on an all-round traverse, to ensure stability when in action.

Soviet 2½-ton truck 6 x 6, Rocket Launcher "Katyusha". The Russians used a variety of trucks to carry the launching rails for their 130-mm rockets, but the Lend-Lease Studebaker was among the most popular. It fired 16 rockets, initiated by electrical impulse, in about 8 to 10 seconds. *Katyusha* was used as a general name for all Soviet rocket projectiles, which ranged from 75-mm to 408-mm. The 130-mm missiles had a range of 6,500 yards and a 48-lb warhead. Like the *Nebelwerfer, Katyusha,* or "Stalin's Organ Pipes", made a noise in flight which earned it this apt nickname. The first Germans to experience its devastating fire were caught in the open as they were moving up for an attack. When the rockets began to howl down they turned and fled. It was not an accurate weapon, but massed batteries made up for this by drenching their target with fire. The Russians, however, claimed that in its first operational use 17 tanks and 15 artillery pieces were knocked out. The mounting and rails weighed 7.1 tons, elevated 15° to 45° and traversed 10° to 20° on the mount.

THE SEA WAR

As the war on land was entering its last desperate struggles, the war at sea was tapering off. The hardest days had been earlier in the war, when German U-boats had stood a good chance of severing Great Britain's sea communications with the rest of the world. The threat had been averted, chiefly by British corvettes, sloops, and frigates. But Germany was working on new designs at the end of the war, and these could have posed the same problem yet again.

Germany's surface forces, although small, were of a high quality in their *matériel,* and continued to worry British naval planners until the great battle-ship *Tirpitz* was put out of the picture. But for this threat, the British naval forces in the Mediterranean could have been strengthened in the critical days of 1942, and the fleet in the Far East made into a major force much earlier than it was.

Insofar as the types of ships are concerned, it is worth noting the decline of the battleship as a capital weapon, and the emergence of the aircraft-carrier in its place. This was to be a fact brought home in the Pacific.

The submarine continued to evolve as a major factor, but it was still severely hampered by its need for air–even with a *Schnorchel,* there was a good chance of the submarine being detected. It might be better to call the boats of this period submersibles rather than sub-marines, reserving the latter word for nuclear-powered boats.

Towards the end of the war, there sprang up a strange tribe of small craft associated with the Allies' needs for invasion purposes, and the Germans' for cheap and easily-obtained ways of countering the Allies' forces, both great and small. Thus were born the assortment of landing craft and midget submarines.

The British aircraft-carrier *Indomitable*. This fleet carrier was one of the six units of the "Illustrious" class, and was launched on March 26, 1940 at the Barrow yards of Vickers-Armstrong. The class was notable for the provision of an armoured hangar, which proved invaluable, especially in the Pacific during 1945. The first four of the class (*Illustrious*, *Victorious*, *Formidable*, and *Indomitable*) displaced 23,000 tons, and the last two (*Implacable* and *Indefatigable*) 26,000 tons, which enabled them to carry 72 aircraft instead of the first four's 36.

The British battleship *Rodney*. This capital ship was launched at the Cammell Laird yards on December 17, 1925, and was armed with nine 16-inch guns. These were, however, disposed oddly, in three triple turrets, all forward. As a result of the Washington Naval Treaty, engine power was low, and this resulted in a truncated stern, giving the unbalanced appearance there. During the war anti-aircraft armament was greatly increased, thirty-two 2-pounders, sixteen 40-mm, and sixty-five 20-mm guns being added.

The German pocket-battleship *Admiral Graf von Spee*. Designed as commerce raiders, the three units of this *Panzerschiffe* class were built to a scaled down battle-cruiser concept, to outrun what they could not outgun, and outgun all other vessels. The design, with six 11-inch guns in a 12,000-ton hull, was an interesting one, but not altogether successful. However, the two units that survived after 1939, *Lützow* (ex-*Deutschland*) and *Admiral Scheer*, remained very considerable threats in the Baltic.

The German heavy cruiser *Admiral Hipper*. Built at the Blohm und Voss yards in Hamburg, *Hipper* was launched on February 6, 1937 and was the fifth and last of Germany's superb heavy cruisers. With eight 8-inch guns, 5-inch armour, and a speed of 32 knots, these were ship-for-ship superior to any British heavy cruiser afloat. *Lützow* had been given to Russia in 1940, and *Blücher* sunk during the invasion of Norway on April 9, 1940, but the other three (*Seydlitz*, *Prinz Eugen*, and *Hipper*), proved very useful in the Baltic in the closing stages of the war.

The British battleship *Duke of York,* one of the five units in the "King George V" class. The others were *King George V, Prince of Wales, Anson,* and *Howe.* The class was designed after Nazi Germany's intentions became clear, and the non-availability of 16-inch mountings, as the result of an agreement of 1935 between Britain, France, Russia, and the United States, meant that a main battery of 14-inch calibre had to be used. Ten of these guns were mounted, and with armour up to 16 inches thick, and a speed of 29 knots, the five "K.G. Fives" were very useful ships.

The British light cruiser *Diadem.* This was one of a second group of five ships in the 16-strong "Dido" class, all launched between 1939 and 1942. Displacing 5,770 tons, *Diadem* had an armament of eight 5.25-inch dual purpose (anti-aircraft and surface) guns in four twin turrets, compared with the ten guns of the first group's ships. Speed was 33 knots, and maximum armour thickness 3 inches. The *Diadem* was launched on August 26, 1942, and spent all her war-time career with the Home Fleet. She was sold to Pakistan in 1956.

The British cruiser *Belfast.* This was a sister ship of *London,* and the two formed the third group of the ten-strong "Southampton" class, launched between 1936 and 1938. The first two groups displaced 9,100 and 9,400 tons, but the third had additional protection (hull bulges and up to $4\frac{1}{2}$ inches of armour) and so displaced 10,000 tons. Armament was twelve 6-inch guns in four triple turrets. Speed was 32 knots. *Belfast* served with the Home Fleet from 1938 to the end of the war, performing notably in the Normandy invasion.

The British Landing Craft, Tank (Rocket). Many such craft were produced by adapting L.C.T.(2)s and (3)s. Provision was also made for quick re-conversion if the need arose. False decks were fitted over the hold, and on this a converted (2) could mount 792 5-inch rockets, and the (3) 1,080. The rockets were fired electrically, in 24 salvoes. Range was fixed at 3,500 yards, and an area of 750 yards by 160 yards was saturated to the density of one rocket per 100 square yards. Another rocket-armed vessel was the Landing Craft, Support (Rocket).

The British frigate *Test*. This was one of the large "River" class of frigates. Early war service had shown corvettes to be too small for ocean escort work, so a new type, soon named frigate, was designed to replace corvettes on the slips. The "River" class was introduced in 1941, and displaced 1,370 tons compared with the average corvette's 950 tons. Speed was not vital in anti-submarine craft, as reflected in the "River" class's 20 knots. Main armament was two 4-inch guns, but more important was the "Hedgehog" anti-submarine weapon.

The British destroyer *Whirlwind*. She was a "W" class destroyer, launched on August 30, 1943. The class had a relatively light anti-aircraft armament (two 40- and eight 20-mm guns), but a main armament of four single 4.7-inch guns and eight 21-inch torpedo tubes. The engines developed 40,000 horsepower, which enabled a top speed of 36¾ knots to be reached. There were eight "W" class ships, and eight in the basically similar "Z" class. Both classes served with the Home Fleet until Germany's surrender.

The British monitor *Erebus*. The design philosophy behind monitors is a simple one: the ship is nothing more than a means of moving heavy guns to the point where they may undertake a shore bombardment. *Erebus* was typical of this idea, with a main armament of two 15-inch guns in a massive turret, made of armour up to 13-inches thick. So that she could close in near to the coast, she had a shallow draught (11 feet), and speed (at 12 knots) was low. *Erebus* was launched on June 16, 1916 and displaced 7,200 tons.

The British Landing Craft, Flak (4). Vessels of this class were adaptations of the L.S.T., and were later redesignated L.C.F. (L.). Twenty-eight of the Mark IV type were built. Displacement was 415 tons and speed a mere 11 knots, but the armament of four 2-pounder and eight 20-mm anti-aircraft guns was heavy for a craft of this size. Some of the earlier L.C.F.s had an armament of up to four 4-inch or eight 2-pounder guns, plus a considerable cannon barrage. Two L.C.F. (2)s and 16 L.C.F. (3)s were built. Draught in the L.C.F. (3) type was only 4½ feet.

The German Schnellboote or E-boat. These were very useful craft, fulfilling much the same functions as the British motor torpedo boats and motor gun boats. The E-boats had a distinct advantage in their larger size and more solid construction. Most were of about 100 tons displacement and armed with two 21-inch torpedo tubes, plus one 40- or 37-mm and five 20-mm guns. Six to eight mines could be carried instead of reload torpedoes. The speed of the various classes differed from 36 to 42 knots, with most capable of about 40 knots.

The German "Biber" type midget submarine. Several types of midget U-boats were designed towards the end of the war, when it was thought that they would be capable of piercing the Allies' U-boat defences and wreaking havoc on the invasion fleets. None of the types was especially successful. The *Biber* type was of 6¼ tons displacement and could make 5 knots underwater, at which speed range was 40 miles. Crew was one and armament two 21-inch torpedoes. Deschimag of Bremen built all the 324 placed in service.

The German Type XXI U-boat. This was the most advanced conventional type developed by Germany, and it could run its diesel engines underwater by use of a *Schnorchel.* Combined with a carefully streamlined hull, without a deck, and an all-welded hull, this allowed a top speed of 16 knots underwater. For silent running there were electric engines, giving a speed of five knots. Submerged displacement was 1,819 tons, and armament six 21-inch tubes with 23 torpedoes. Luckily for the Allies, none saw active service.

The British "T" class submarine. This class, some 51 boats strong, displaced 1,575 tons submerged, and carried an armament of 10 or 11 tubes and one 4-inch gun. Submerged speed was nine knots. Boats of the class served in home waters, the Mediterranean, and the Far East with considerable success. War experience soon showed that more range was needed, and some of the ballast tanks were turned into extra fuel tanks. The type was superseded on the stocks by the "A" class in 1944, but the boats of this class were too late to see Pacific service.

THE AIR WAR

The greatest technical strides made in the war were those in the field of aeronautics and associated areas. In 1939, aircraft were still relatively simple: uncomplicated airframe, piston engine, relatively light armament, and few technical aids. By 1945 aircraft were far larger and heavier, making considerable use of advances in aerodynamics, possessed of much heavier and more sophisticated offensive and defensive weapons, and advanced electronic aids to navigation and interception.

The typical fighter of 1939 was powered by a 1,000-hp engine, capable of about 350 mph at its optimum altitude (in the region of 15,000 feet), with a service ceiling of about 32,000 feet and range of 400 miles, and an armament of light machine guns and the occasional cannon.

By 1945, fighters were over twice as heavy, at some 10,000 lbs, powered by massive engines developing about 2,500 hp, able to reach 450 mph at rated altitude (20,000+ feet), with a service ceiling in excess of 40,000 feet and a range of over 1,000 miles, and an armament of heavy machine guns, large calibre cannon, bombs, and rockets.

Bombers had also undergone an enormous transformation. To take only the example of the heavy bomber: in 1939, a typical "heavy" bomber could carry a load of 7,000 lbs of bombs at under 230 mph for under 1,000 miles. Defensive armament was a matter of only five or six light machine guns. Loaded weight was up to about 30,000 lbs and power was provided by two 1,000-hp engines.

1945 bombers were radically different. Apart from electronic aids such as H2S, Gee, and Oboe, the bomb-load had doubled to about 15,000 lbs maximum, and speed had increased to about 290 mph, with a range of 2,000 miles or more available. Defensive armament had increased, in British bombers up to eight light machine guns, in American machines up to 14 heavy machine guns, and in German aircraft up to two cannon and five heavy machine guns.

Apart from the growth of established classes, new classes, such as fighter-bombers, night fighters, and specialised ground attack aircraft, not to mention anti-submarine and anti-shipping machines, made their appearance, and even took over from such types as interceptors and light bombers in importance. Aircraft capable of undertaking several rôles were becoming ever more important.

Finally, the closing stages of the war saw a revolution in aircraft propulsion. There were oddities such as the Messerschmitt 163 rocket interceptor. And there were truer portents of the future in turbojet-propelled types such as the Me 262.

△ *Best all round fighter of World War II, the beautiful North American P-51 Mustang. Furthest from the camera is a P-51C, with the original framed canopy, with three P-51D's, the first model to feature a blister canopy. All four would have been powered by American Packard-built Merlin inline engines.*

The British Bristol Beaufighter Torpedo-Fighter X.
Derived from the Beaufort torpedo bomber, the Beaufighter heavy fighter first flew in July 1937. The type had been ordered for the R.A.F. even before it flew, and the first production models entered service in September 1940. By the end of the year, several examples had been fitted with primitive Airborne Interception radar for the night fighter rôle, a rôle in which the Beaufighter continued to give much valuable service. In the summer of 1941, the Merlin powered Mark IIF entered service, to be superseded in 1942 by the Mark VI. This could carry rockets or a torpedo. The last major model produced was the Mark X, the best anti-shipping strike fighter of the war.

The British de Havilland Mosquito Fighter-Bomber VI. The Mosquito had a simple and unique bonded wood construction pioneered by the manufacturers. The prototype flew in November 1940, and production models started to enter service in July 1941. The first three production models were the Photographic Reconnaissance I, Night Fighter II, and Bomber IV, the last of which was unarmed, being faster than contemporary German fighters. Next came the F.B. VI, which was built in greater numbers than any other model. This was followed by the F.B. XVIII, armed with a 57-mm gun. The B. IX and XVI, then followed, while the N.F. XII, XIII, XVII, XIX, and 30 completed the night fighters.

The British Gloster Meteor III.
This was Britain's first jet fighter, and the only Allied jet to see service in the war. The prototype, which had benefited considerably from experience gained with the Gloster E.28/39, Britain's first jet aircraft, flew on March 5, 1943, and was powered by two Halford turbojets. Production models, powered by Rolls-Royce Welland engines, entered service in July 1944, and were soon in action against V-1 flying bombs. The speed of the Meteor I was only 410 mph, but the Mark III, which entered service at the beginning of 1945, had Derwents, which had 300 lbs thrust per engine more. This boosted top speed up to 493 mph. Mark III's started to serve in North-West Europe from spring 1945.

The British Hawker Tempest V. This excellent fighter was conceived as an updated version of the Typhoon, which had entered service in July 1941. The new Tempest featured a better canopy, stronger tail surfaces, a more powerful engine, and a thin laminar-flow elliptical wing, and flew for the first time on February 24, 1943. Various engines (Napier Sabre II and IV, Bristol Centaurus, and Rolls-Royce Griffon) were tried, but only the Marks II (Centaurus) and V (Sabre II) were persevered with. The Mark V entered service first, in January 1944, and proved a worthy companion for the Typhoon. Fixed armament comprised four 20-mm cannon, and eight rockets or 2,000 lbs of bombs could be carried, giving a powerful attack capability.

The British Hawker Tempest II. As noted above, this was the version of the Tempest using the 2,500-hp Bristol Centaurus V or VI radial. With its engine enclosed in a neat cowling, the Tempest II had a pleasing and aggressive look to it. Trouble with vibration somewhat hampered early trials, and production did not start until August 1944, deliveries to the Royal Air Force only commencing three months after the war. The Tempest II was a good aircraft, however, having the same armament as the Mark V, and better performance, with a top speed 6 mph greater at a lower altitude of 15,000 feet, a climb to that altitude 30 seconds faster, at 4 minutes 30 seconds, and 110 miles extra range, at 1,640 miles.

The British Supermarine Spitfire 21. This was the final war-time version of Britain's most famous fighter, but it appeared in R.A.F. service just too late to see service. Although superficially similar to its predecessors, the Spitfire 21 had undergone a structural redesign, the most obvious sign of which was a new wing. This was of increased area and so of a different shape to the distinctive elliptical planform of the earlier models. The powerplant was a Rolls-Royce Griffon inline, top speed 454 mph, ceiling 43,500 feet, and range 880 miles. The Mark 22 was similar, but featured a blister canopy and redesigned tail surfaces, which also appeared on the last Spitfire, the Mark 24, which had zero-length rocket rails and short-barrelled cannon.

The British Avro Lancaster III. The most famous British bomber of the war, the Lancaster had its origins in the unsuccessful two-engined Manchester. The prototype flew for the first time on January 9, 1941, and service deliveries started in December. The basic Mark I, of which more than 3,500 were built, was supplemented in 1942 by the Mark X, Canadian-built Mark I's using the American Packard-built Merlin. The Mark II featured Bristol Hercules radial engines, as it was feared that Merlin output could not match demand, but the fears proved groundless and only 300 Mark II's were built. The Mark III was generally similar to the Mark I but had Packard Merlin engines. About 3,000 of this second major mark were built.

The American Consolidated B-24 Liberator. Although not as celebrated as its fellow bomber the Fortress, the Liberator was a very successful aircraft, and served in a much wider variety of rôles: bomber, maritime reconnaissance bomber, and transport. Noteworthy features were the high aspect ratio, low drag wing, the large fuselage, and the mounting of the wing at the shoulder position, which did not take up much fuselage space and thus allowed easy conversion of the type into a transport. The Liberator also had a tricycle undercarriage, made desirable by the wing's position. The Liberator was a rugged machine, possessed of exceptional range (over 3,000 miles maximum), which suited it well for maritime rôles.

The American Douglas A-20 Havoc. Known to the Royal Air Force as the Boston, this was the most successful American attack aircraft of the war. The type's direct ancestor was the DB-7 light bomber, many of which were ordered by France and taken over by Britain as Bostons after the fall of that unhappy country. The first American A-20's were converted to night fighters and reconnaissance machines, and thereafter the type served in a multitude of rôles: attack bomber, reconnaissance, heavy fighter, night fighter, night intruder, and maritime strike machine. Armament carried could comprise a torpedo or up to 4,000 lbs of bombs, plus a 37-mm cannon and a mixture of 20-mm cannon and .5-inch machine guns. A total of 7,385 was built.

The American Boeing B-17G Flying Fortress. The American equivalent of the British Lancaster, the Flying Fortress was designed as a high altitude precision day bomber. The prototype flew on July 28, 1935, and after trials the test aircraft were accepted for service as the B-17 and 17A. The first production model, the 17B, was phased out of building early in 1940 in favour of the more powerful 17C. By 1942 the generally similar 17D was in production. The 17E had the new tail design and a rear turret, and the 17F included only minor improvements. Finally came the 17G, which incorporated the most important modification deemed necessary after combat experience, a chin turret. The 17G could carry 17,600 lbs of bombs.

The American Northrop P-61 Black Widow. This was the first U.S. aircraft designed as a night fighter. The prototype first flew on May 21, 1942, and service aircraft were operating over North-West Europe by 1944. This large twin-engined, twin boom machine had an armament of four 20-mm cannon and four .5-inch machine guns, and a crew of three. As the nose was occupied by the radar antenna, the cannon were fitted in the belly of the aircraft, and the machine guns in a remotely-controlled turret on top of the fuselage. The top turret was deleted after 37 P-61A's had been delivered, only to be restored on the last 250 P-51B's, which also had provision for four 1,600-lb bombs on underwing points.

The American Martin B-26 Marauder. The first example of this medium bomber flew on November 25, 1940, and the type entered service quickly. The B-26B introduced a twin-gun rear turret. The Marauder had a high wing loading, and was thus somewhat tricky to fly, but in the hands of a competent pilot it was an excellent machine, suffering very few losses in the closing stages of the war in Europe. The final model of the Marauder, the B-26G, could carry up to 4,000 lbs of bombs, had a machine gun armament of eleven .5-inch guns, a top speed of 283 mph, and a range of 1,100 miles. Surprisingly, in a relatively small aircraft, there were seven crew members. A total of 5,157 Marauders was built before production ceased.

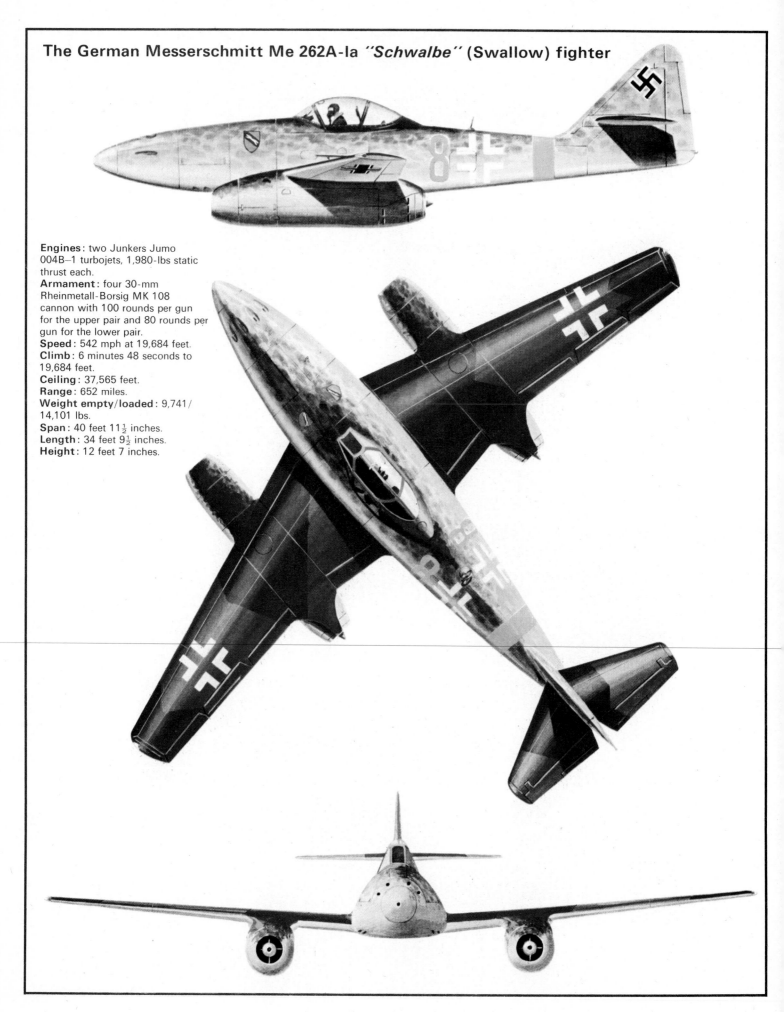

The German Messerschmitt Me 262A-la *"Schwalbe"* (Swallow) fighter

Engines: two Junkers Jumo 004B–1 turbojets, 1,980-lbs static thrust each.
Armament: four 30-mm Rheinmetall-Borsig MK 108 cannon with 100 rounds per gun for the upper pair and 80 rounds per gun for the lower pair.
Speed: 542 mph at 19,684 feet.
Climb: 6 minutes 48 seconds to 19,684 feet.
Ceiling: 37,565 feet.
Range: 652 miles.
Weight empty/loaded: 9,741/ 14,101 lbs.
Span: 40 feet $11\frac{1}{2}$ inches.
Length: 34 feet $9\frac{1}{2}$ inches.
Height: 12 feet 7 inches.

The German Messerschmitt Me 163B-la *"Komet"* interceptor

Engine: one Walter HWK 109-509-A-2 rocket motor, 3,750-lbs static thrust.
Armament: two 30-mm Rheinmetall-Borsig MK 108 cannon with 60 rounds per gun, plus 24 5-cm R4M rockets underwing or 4 R4M rockets in each wing, firing vertically upwards.
Speed: 596 mph between 10,000 and 30,000 feet.
Climb: 2 minutes 36 seconds to 30,000 feet.
Ceiling: 39,500 feet.
Endurance: 8 minutes.
Weight empty/loaded: 4,200/9,500 lbs.
Span: 30 feet 7 inches.
Length: 18 feet 8 inches.
Height: 9 feet.

The American North American B-25G Mitchell. This medium bomber was ordered "off the drawing board", and the first example flew on August 19, 1940, production of the B-25A getting under way swiftly. By the end of 1941 the B-25B was in production. This had an improved armament. The 25C and 25D were basically similar, although some examples had provision for a torpedo. The next production model was the celebrated 25G, which had a "solid" nose mounting a 75-mm gun for attacking shipping and ground targets. The 25H carried a phenomenal armament: a lighter 75-mm gun, fourteen .5-inch machine guns, and a torpedo or 3,200 lbs of bombs. Finally came the definitive 25J, of which 4,318 were built.

The American North American P-51D. This most celebrated of American fighters was flown for the first time in October 1940. As the machine was the result of British enquiries and requirements, it incorporated the lessons of European combat experience. The original P-51 and 51A models were good machines, but the limitations of the Allison engine used meant that it was only at low level that the P-51 excelled. But in 1942 it was suggested that the Merlin should be fitted to the Mustang, and so was born the best all round fighter of the war. The Merlin-engined P-51B still had the framed canopy, however, and it was not until the advent of the P-51D that the blister canopy was introduced.

The American Republic P-47N Thunderbolt. This was, with the Mustang, The United States' most famous fighter, and was the largest and heaviest single-engined fighter of World War II. The prototype, the XP-47B, flew on May 6, 1941 and was immediately ordered into production, deliveries commencing in November. The 47C featured a ventral fuel tank and was longer; the 47D, 12,602 of which were built, had provision for underwing stores, and more importantly, introduced the blister canopy. Several experimental models followed, one of which attained a speed of 504 mph, and the next production model was the 47M, a special sprint model capable of 470 mph. Final model was the 47N, which had a larger wing, and was strengthened for heavier loads.

The German Focke Wulf Ta 152H. Derived from the long-nosed inline-engined Fw 190D, the 152 series was the ultimate in German piston-engined fighter designs. Although the Fw 190 had been designed with a radial engine, the D series was fitted with a Junkers Jumo inline, while still maintaining the appearance of a radial-engined type, and proved immensely successful. The Ta 152 series initially differed little from the 190D-9, but the B introduced an engine-mounted 30-mm cannon and was produced from August 1944. The 152C, however, was powered by a Daimler-Benz engine, and was the only 152 model to see service. Final model was the 152H, intended as a high altitude interceptor, and capable of 472 mph.

The German Heinkel 177 "Greif". This was Germany's best attempt at a strategic heavy bomber, but did not turn out to be a success. The prototype flew in November 1939, but trouble was soon experienced with the engines. These were of an unusual and advanced design, with two Daimler-Benz 601 inlines coupled to a single crankshaft and driving a single propeller. One of these double engines was fitted in each wing, and difficulties, never fully eradicated, were encountered with cooling problems. The engines, in fact, had an alarming tendency to catch fire in the air. The best model was the 177A-5, which had a top speed of 295 mph, and could carry a bomb-load of 13,225 lbs. Range was 2,260 miles maximum.

The German Junkers 88G-1. The Junkers 88 series was Germany's most versatile aircraft of World War II, serving as a bomber, ground attack, reconnaissance, and day and night fighter aircraft. The prototype flew in December 1936, production of the basic bomber version starting in 1938 and deliveries in 1939. The type's excellent performance soon recommended it as an all-purpose machine, and it was quickly pressed into service in other rôles. The first night fighter series was the 88C, the first examples of which appeared at the end of 1940. But the ever-increasing numbers and efficiency of British night bombers led to introduction of the heavily-armed 88G series in the summer of 1944.

The German Heinkel 219 "Uhu". This was undoubtedly Germany's best night fighter of the war. It was designed in 1940 as a high altitude interceptor, but in 1942 was altered into a night fighter when the German air ministry put out a requirement for such an aircraft. The prototype flew on November 15, 1942 and trials confirmed the early promise of the type. Production started in August 1943, and combat success soon followed the type's entry into service. Of particular interest was the *"Shräge Musik"* (Jazz Music) installation. This comprised two 30-mm cannon mounted in the fuselage and firing obliquely forwards and upwards. With this, the pilot could position his machine below and behind a bomber, in its blind spot.

The German Messerschmitt 410A. This machine was derived from the unsuccessful Me 210 of 1941, which was intended to complement the Bf 110 in the fighter-bomber and reconnaissance rôles. Despite its neat and purposeful looks, however, the 210 was a total failure, no modifications making any significant improvement. Production ceased after 325 had been built. After extensive redesign, the type emerged as the 410, which was a better, but not good, aircraft. A total of 1,913 was built, in three main versions: the 410A-1 as a fighter-bomber (4,400-lb bomb-load), the 410A-2 as a heavy fighter (additional two 20-mm and a 50-mm cannon), and 410A-3 as a reconnaissance machine with cameras and fuel in the bomb bay.

The German Arado 234 "Blitz". The only jet bomber to see service in World War II, the *Blitz* was a very advanced design. The prototype was completed in the early winter of 1941, but the non-availability of engines meant that the first flight did not take place until June 15, 1943. The early models had a somewhat unusual undercarriage arrangement: the aircraft took off from a large three-wheeled trolley, which was jettisoned after take-off, and landed on three retractable skids. By the time that the 234B series entered production, however, the type had been provided with a more conventional retractable tricycle undercarriage. Some later development models had four engines, mounted singly or in pairs.

The German Heinkel 162 "Salamander". This unusual jet fighter was designed as a last ditch *"Volksjäger"* or People's Fighter, to be flown by *Hitlerjugend* and the like. It took only ten weeks to design and build, and was constructed of wood and other non-strategic materials, the B.M.W. turbojet being mounted on top of the fuselage piggy-back fashion. Deliveries began in February 1945, and by the time of Germany's surrender, 116 examples had been handed over. The design was structurally defective, however, and also extremely difficult to fly. Maximum speed was 522 mph at 19,700 feet, and the armament of the 162A-2 illustrated was two 20-mm cannon.

The Russian Yakovlev 9. This was the most widely-produced of any Yakovlev fighter, and was an excellent machine, robust, easy to fly, and adequately armed. It was a progressive modification of the Yak 7, from which it differed principally in having redesigned wings, with extra fuel tanks, and the cockpit placed further back along the fuselage. The type went into production in early 1942, and was first encountered by the Germans over Stalingrad in October. In 1943, two new models appeared: the 9D, with reduced armament and increased fuel for escort duties, and the 9T, of which there were two versions. One had a 37-mm cannon and a 12.7-mm machine gun, and the other a 75-mm gun.

The Russian Lavochkin 5FN. Early in 1942, the Russians decided to improve the performance of the Lavochkin-Gorbunov-Gudkov 3 by replacing its 1,100-hp inline engine with a 1,640-hp radial. The whole of the nose and front fuselage had to be redesigned, but the new fighter turned out to have a good performance and was placed in production in time for the first service models, the La-5, to see action at Stalingrad in 1942 and the improved La-5FN at Kursk in July 1943. This latter had a more powerful engine and detail improvements, such as a cut down rear fuselage to improve the pilot's view. Armament was two 20-mm cannon, and speed 402 mph at sea level, very useful as most Eastern Front flying was at low level.

The Russian Petlyakov 2. This was one of the best Russian aircraft of the war, and indeed one of the best light bombers to see service with any of the combatants. The type entered service in 1941, and its good performance soon ensured that it was used on ground attack and reconnaissance missions, as well as light bombing. It was also used as a night fighter. With two 1,100-hp Klimov inline engines, the Pe-2 had a top speed of 335 mph at 16,400 feet, and a range of 1,200 miles. Armament consisted of 2,200 lbs of bombs, plus one 12.7-mm and four 7.62-mm machine guns. A development for night fighting, the Pe-3, was introduced in 1943. This had a solid nose with four machine guns, and a shorter canopy with a dorsal turret.

The Russian Ilyushin 2m3 was the best aircraft produced by Russia during the war, and one of the classic military aircraft of all time. Designed only for ground attack, the Il-2 entered service in 1941 as a single-seater. Armament comprised a bomb-load of up to 1,325 lbs, or eight 82-mm rockets and 880 lbs of bombs, plus two 20-mm cannon and two 7.62-mm machine guns. It was soon realised that some rear defence was necessary, however, and a second crew member was added in the Il-2m3 of late 1942. The gunner had a 12.7-mm machine gun. The most important factor in the Il-2's construction was the manufacture of the whole of the forward fuselage from some 1,500 lbs of armour plate.

The American Bell P-63 Kingcobra. The Kingcobra was a development of the P-39 Airacobra, and the first prototype flew on December 7, 1942. The type did not suit American requirements, however, and most of the 3,303 aircraft built were supplied to the Free French and Russian air forces under Lend-Lease. The Russians in particular found the aircraft just right for their low-level tactics, as had been the P-39, and were very pleased with the machine. Armament comprised one 37-mm cannon, four .5-inch machine guns, and up to 1,500 lbs of bombs. Speed was 410 mph. An unusual design feature was the fact that the engine was behind the pilot, driving the propeller via an extension shaft, in an effort to increase manoeuvrability.

CHAPTER 142

East Prussia invaded

Soviet 203-mm howitzers
prepares to fire the opening
barrage of the final offensive of
the war in the East. The
Russians massed 43 divisions of
artillery to give the 1st
Belorussian and 1st Ukrainian
Fronts a superiority of nearly
eight to one in guns and
mortars.

January 12, 1945 saw the Red Army pour out in a great torrent over the bridge-heads it had won the previous summer on the left bank of the Vistula. Two days later it was assaulting the German positions on the Narew and the defences of Eastern Prussia which, three months earlier, had defied the efforts of Zakharov and Chernyakhovsky. Two months later Konev crossed the Oder both above and below Breslau (Wrocław), Zhukov reached it between Frankfurt and Küstrin (Kostrzyn), Rokossovsky was at its mouth and Vasilevsky was about to demolish Königsberg.

To the Wehrmacht, the Third Reich, and Hitler, defeated also on the Western Front, this was the death blow. It was to mean the end of nine centuries of conquest, occupation, and civilisation by the Germans of the whole area between the Oder-Neisse line and the eastern frontiers of Germany as drawn up at Versailles. On May 8, 1945 nearly eight million inhabitants of East Prussia, Pomerania, and the borderland between Brandenburg and Silesia fled their homes before the invading Soviets. More than three and a half million more Germans were to be driven out of these same areas between 1945 and 1950. The defeat of Germany's military might was thus to bring about the

greatest movement of peoples since the collapse of the Roman Empire and the invasions by the Germans, Iranians, and Huns in the 5th Century A.D.

109 divisions in the West . . .

We turn now to the forces with which Germany fought the Red Army in the last stage of their merciless duel.

At the turn of the year O.K.W. had 288 divisions, including 45 Panzer and *Panzergrenadier*. This number does not, however, include the divisions in course of formation under *Reichsführer* Heinrich Himmler, C.-in-C. of the *Ersatzheer* since the attempt on Hitler's life of July 20, 1944.

124 of these divisions were under O.K.W.:

O.B. West (France) under Rundstedt:	74
O.B. *Süd* (Italy) under Kesselring:	24
O.B. *Süd-Ost* (Bosnia and Croatia) under Weichs:	9
Crete, Rhodes, and dependencies:	2
20th Mountain Army (Norway) under Rendulic:	15

Take away from this total the *Süd-Ost* forces fighting the Yugoslav Liberation Army and the six divisions of Colonel-General Rendulic keeping the Russians out of Narvik in the area of Lyngenfjord, and we see that the Western fronts between them were engaging 109 German divisions, or some 40 per cent of Germany's military strength at the end of 1944.

. . . and 164 in the East against massive opposition

This gave O.K.H. 164 divisions with which to fight the Red Army on a front running from the Drava at Barcs on its right to the Gulf of Riga in the area of Tukums on its left. Army Group "South" in Hungary (General Wöhler) had 38 divisions, including 15 Panzer or *Panzergrenadier*. In the Kurland bridgehead Colonel-General Schörner had 27 divisions, including three Panzer. This left 99 divisions for Army Groups "A" and "Centre" to hold the front between the southern slopes of the Carpathians and Memel on the Baltic.

▽ *A troop of SU-76 assault guns grinds across the frost-covered plains of north Germany.*

Gehlen's warning

When Major-General Gehlen reported his conclusion that a powerful enemy offensive was imminent against Army Groups "A" and "Centre", Guderian expressed his dissatisfaction with the deployment of the German forces. He wanted Kurland to be evacuated and no more reinforcements to be sent to the Hungarian theatre of operations. In his opinion, the essential thing was to protect Germany from the invasion now threatening her and, to this end, to keep the enemy out of the approaches to upper Silesia, to Breslau, Berlin, Danzig, and Königsberg.

He put this to Hitler and his O.K.W. colleagues at Ziegenberg on December 24. But, as we have pointed out before, Gehlen's report left the Führer incredulous. Worse still, when Guderian had got back to Zossen, south of Berlin, where O.K.H. had moved after the evacuation of Rastenburg, he was informed that during his return journey he had been deprived of IV S.S. Panzer Corps, which was now to go to the Hungarian front. The corps was in Army Group "Centre" reserve behind the Narew, and this group's mobile reserves between the Carpathians and the Baltic were thus reduced at a stroke from 14 to 12 divisions, or, if they were all up to strength, by 1,350 armoured vehicles.

Guderian warns Hitler and Jodl

In spite of this snub, Guderian went back to Ziegenberg on January 1, 1945 in the hope of getting O.K.W. to see things his way. In his view, the centre of gravity of German strategy had to be brought back to the Eastern Front. But when Himmler was about to unleash the *"Nordwind"* offensive which was to replace *"Herbstnebel"*, with Saverne as its objective, Jodl was as unenthusiastic about Guderian's ideas as Hitler had been. "We have no right," he pointed out to him, "to give up the initiative we have just regained;

The German *Flakpanzer* 38(t) self-propelled A.A. mounting

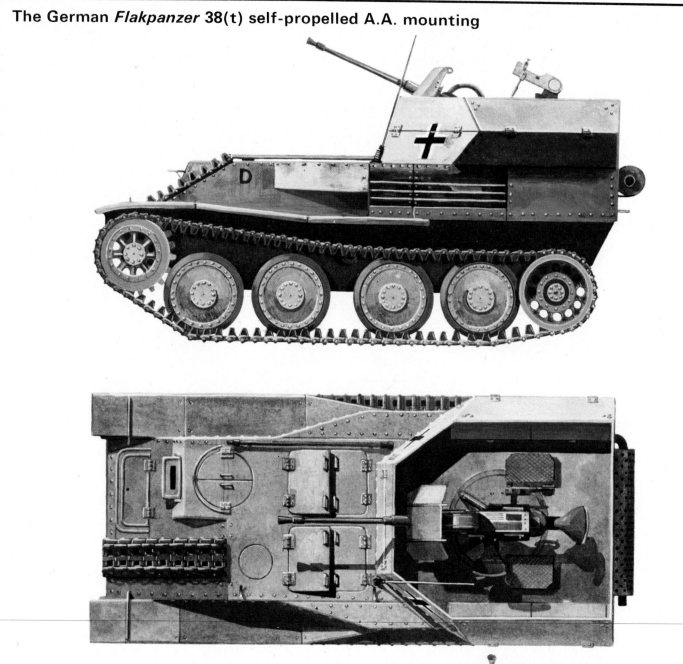

Weight: 9.8 tons.
Crew: 4.
Armament: one 2-cm *Flak* 38 L/55 cannon.
Armour: hull nose and front 25+25-mm, glacis 25-mm, sides 30-mm, rear 12-mm, decking 10-mm, and belly 8-mm.
Engine: one EPA Model III inline, 125-hp.
Speed: 25 mph.
Range: 94 miles on roads and 64 miles cross-country.
Length: 17 feet.
Width: 6 feet 9 inches.
Height: 7 feet 10 inches.

we can always give ground in the East, but never in the West."

Shown the door for the second time, Guderian nevertheless made a third attempt to see Hitler to remind him of his responsibilities towards the Eastern Front. As the days passed without any decision being made, the Russians completed their preparations and, according to Gehlen's reckoning, their "steamroller", now building up its pressure, had at least: 231 infantry divisions, 22 tank corps, 29 independent tank brigades, and three cavalry corps, supported by air forces that the Luftwaffe could not hope to match.

After taking the advice of Colonel-Generals Harpe and Reinhardt, commanders of Army Groups "A" and "Centre", against which the threat was mounting, Guderian drew up the following programme and presented it to Hitler on January 9:

1. Evacuation of the Kurland bridgehead.
2. Transfer to the East of a number of armoured units then fighting on the Western Front.
3. Abandonment of the line of the Narew and withdrawal of Army Group "Centre" to the East Prussian frontier, which was shorter and better protected.
4. Evacuation of the Army Group "A" salient between the bridge at Baranów and Magnuszew through which, according to Gehlen, 91 Soviet infantry divisions, one cavalry corps, 13 tank corps, and nine tank brigades were ready to break out.

In presenting these proposals, Guderian might have had in mind Jodl's opinion that some ground could still be sacrificed in the East. But he had hardly put before Hitler the comparative table of opposing forces which accompanied the plan, than the Führer broke out into a spate of abuse and sarcasm. A violent scene then took place which Guderian has described as follows:

"Gehlen had very carefully prepared the documentation on the enemy situation, with maps and diagrams which gave a clear idea of the respective strengths. Hitler flew into a rage when I showed them to him, called them 'absolutely stupid' and demanded that I send their author immediately to a lunatic asylum. I too became angry then. 'This is General Gehlen's work,' I said to Hitler. 'He is one of my best staff officers. I wouldn't have submitted it to you if I hadn't first agreed it myself. If you demand that General Gehlen be put into an asylum, then send me to one too!' I curtly refused to carry out Hitler's order to relieve Gehlen of his post. The storm then calmed down. But no good came of it from a military point of view. Harpe's and Reinhardt's proposals were turned down to the accompaniment of the expected odious remarks about generals for whom 'manoeuvre' only meant 'withdraw to the next rearward position'. This was all very unpleasant."

What threat?

As in Hitler's eyes the Soviet threat was insignificant, not to say non-existent, the measures to meet it proposed by Guderian were therefore completely meaningless. A strictly logical conclusion, such as madmen are liable to arrive at after starting from radically wrong premises, led Hitler to give Guderian this meagre food for thought for his return journey to Zossen: "The Eastern Front must fend for itself and make do with what it has got." Could it be that Guderian was right when he said that Hitler the Austrian and Jodl the Bavarian were indifferent to the threat to Prussia? That might be somewhat far-fetched, but one might equally well suppose that Guderian the Prussian was ready to accept defeat in the West if the 6th *Panzerarmee*'s reinforcements were to be taken out of the Ardennes and given to him to block the Soviet advance towards Berlin. The least we can say is that events confirmed this latter assumption.

In any event it is clear that, reasoning *a priori* as was his custom and despite always being contradicted by events, Hitler took it that Stalin's intention was to deploy his main effort in the Danube basin towards Vienna, the second capital of the Reich, then Munich. On the other hand, after allowing IX S.S. Mountain Corps to become encircled in the so-called fortress of Budapest, it now seemed to Hitler that he should extricate it again as a matter of urgency.

So if the Eastern Front was required to go it alone, the Führer did not give any priority to dealing with Soviet advances towards Königsberg and Berlin or providing any of the resources necessary to stop them.

△ General I. D. Chernyakhovsky, one of the Red Army's brightest stars and commander of the 3rd Belorussian Front until his death in action on February 18.

△ Marshal of the Soviet Union A. M. Vasilevsky, who assumed command of the 3rd Belorussian Front on Chernyakhovsky's death. He was on the spot to co-ordinate the final attacks of the 1st Baltic and 3rd Belorussian Fronts in the crushing of East Prussia.

△ *A German freighter on the run from Danzig is caught by the Red Air Force. Though Hitler's "stand and fight" orders severely hampered the garrisons along the Baltic coast, they received heroic support from the navy. Warships gave close support, and the merchant marine evacuated over two million refugees.*

German strength

On January 12, 1945 German forces were deployed between the Carpathians and the Baltic as follows:

1. Army Group "A" (Colonel-General J. Harpe), with the 1st *Panzerarmee* (Colonel-General G. Heinrici), 17th Army (General F. Schulz), 4th *Panzerarmee* (General F. Gräser), and 9th Army (General S. von Lüttwitz).
2. Army Group "Centre" (Colonel-General G. Reinhardt), with the 2nd Army (Colonel-General W. Weiss), 4th Army (General F. Hossbach), and 3rd *Panzerarmee* (Colonel-General . E. Raus).

The Soviet steamroller

1. Enormous manpower

On January 1, 1945 *Stavka*'s strength, according to Field-Marshal von Manstein, was as follows: 527 infantry and 43 artillery divisions, and 302 tank and mechanised brigades, totalling 5,300,000 men, to the Germans' 164 divisions (1,800,000 men) on the Eastern Front.

2. The JS-3 tank

In the last six-month period, Soviet armoured strength had increased from 9,000 to about 13,400 vehicles, in spite of battle losses. This was all the more remarkable in that the Russians had changed over from the heavy KV-85 to the Stalin tank. This weighed 45 tons and its 122-mm gun was the most powerful tank gun of the war. It had a 600-hp diesel engine, a range of 120 miles, and a top speed of 25 mph. The Soviets also continued to build self-propelled guns, and in particular their SU-85, 100, and 152 vehicles were to take heavy toll of both German permanent and field fortifications.

3. Zhukov's and Konev's enormous resources

If we refer to Alexander Werth's version of *The Great Patriotic War*, Volume 5, we see that *Stavka* allotted to Marshals Zhukov and Konev, commanders of the 1st Belorussian and 1st Ukrainian Fronts

respectively, the following forces:

1. 160 infantry divisions;
2. 32,143 guns and mortars;
3. 6,460 tanks and self-propelled guns; and
4. 4,772 aircraft.

The air forces were divided into two air armies, one to each front. The 16th Air Army (General S. I. Rudenko) was under Marshal Zhukov and the 2nd (General S. A. Krasovsky) under Marshal Konev. *Stavka* had thus done things well and the 1st Belorussian and 1st Ukrainian Fronts had a superiority over the German Army Group "A", according to Werth, of:

(a) 5.5 to 1 in men;
(b) 7.8 to 1 in guns and mortars;
(c) 5.7 to 1 in armoured vehicles; and
(d) 17.7 to 1 in aircraft.

If we realise that the superiority of the 2nd and 3rd Belorussian Fronts (respectively under Marshal Rokossovsky and General Chernyakhovsky) must have been similar, it will be realised that, rather than trying to create a bogey with which to frighten Hitler, Gehlen was on the contrary somewhat modest in his calculations.

Churchill urges Stalin on

The start of the Soviet fourth winter offensive had been fixed for January 20. In fact, it started on the 12th on the 1st Ukrainian Front as the result of an urgent approach to Stalin by Churchill. When he got back from S.H.A.E.F. on January 6, a visit to which we shall refer again, the British Prime Minister sent a very detailed telegram to the Kremlin in these terms:

"The battle in the West is very heavy and, at any time, large decisions may be called for from the Supreme Command. You know yourself from your own experience how very anxious the position is when a very broad front has to be defended after temporary loss of the initiative. It is General Eisenhower's great desire and need to know in outline what you plan to do, as this obviously affects all his and our major decisions. Our Envoy, Air Chief Marshal Tedder, was last night reported weather-bound in Cairo. His journey has been much delayed through no fault of yours. In case he has not reached you yet, I shall be grateful if you can tell me whether we can count on a major Russian offensive on the Vistula front, or elsewhere, during January, with any other points you may care to mention. I shall not pass this most secret information to anyone except Field Marshal Brooke and General Eisenhower, and only under conditions of the utmost secrecy. I regard the matter as urgent."

Approached in these terms, Stalin did not have to be asked twice. Before 24 hours had passed, he replied to Churchill in exceptionally warm terms. Only the weather conditions, he said, preventing the Red Army from taking advantage of its superior strength in artillery and aircraft, were holding back the start of the offensive:

"Still, in view of our Allies' position on the Western Front, GHQ of the Supreme Command have decided to complete preparations at a rapid rate and, regardless of weather, to launch large-scale offensive operations along the entire Central Front not later than the second half of January. Rest assured we shall do all in our power to support the valiant forces of our Allies."

In his memoirs Churchill thought: "It was a fine deed of the Russians and their chief to hasten their vast offensive,

△ *Marshal of the Soviet Union Georgi K. Zhukov. After his conspicuous part in the defence of "Mother Russia" he was now heading the Russian advance to Berlin right across the centre of Poland: south of Warsaw, via Lódź and Poznań, to Oder between Frankfurt and Küstrin.*

△ *Colonel-General N. I. Krylov, commander of the Russian 5th Army, in the 3rd Belorussian Front led by the brilliant General I. D. Chernyakhovsky.*

no doubt at a heavy cost in life."

We would agree with him, though not with Boris Telpukhovsky of the Moscow Academy of Sciences, who in 1959 was inspired to write as follows about this episode in Allied relations:

"In December 1944 on the Western Front the Hitler troops launched an offensive in the Ardennes. With the relatively weak forces at their disposal they were able to make a break-through, which put the Anglo-American command in a difficult position: it even began to look as though there would be a second Dunkirk. As a result on January 6 Churchill approached Stalin with a request for help for the troops fighting in the West."

After quoting from the two telegrams given above, he concludes: "Faithful to undertakings given to his Allies and unlike the ruling Anglo-Americans, who knowingly and willingly delayed the opening of the Second Front, the Soviet Government brought forward the starting date of their offensive from January 20 to 12."

In the face of these statements by the Soviet historian, it must be pointed out that ten days before January 6, Hitler had personally acknowledged in the presence of his generals at Ziegenberg that Operation *"Herbstnebel"* had failed. Twelve days previously Patton had freed Bastogne and it was even longer since the ghost of a new Dunkirk had been

laid once and for all. It should also be remembered that the sending of Air Chief-Marshal Tedder, Eisenhower's second-in-command at S.H.A.E.F., to Moscow was decided before the start of the German offensive in the Ardennes and that his presence there was aimed at co-ordinating the final operations of the Allies in the West with those of the Soviets coming from the East, and to arrange their link-up in the heart of Germany. This was Eisenhower's version as given in his memoirs. Not only does this version seem more acceptable but it is confirmed by President Roosevelt's message to Stalin dated December 24:

"In order that all of us may have information essential to our coordination of effort, I wish to direct General Eisenhower to send a fully qualified officer of his staff to Moscow to discuss with you Eisenhower's situation on the Western Front and its relation to the Eastern Front. We will maintain complete secrecy.

"It is my hope that you will see this officer from General Eisenhower's staff and arrange to exchange with him information that will be of mutual benefit. The situation in Belgium is not bad but we have arrived at the time to talk of the next phase . . . An early reply to this proposal is requested in view of the emergency."

On that same day Churchill, who "did not consider the situation in the West bad", pointed out to his Soviet

▽ While Zhukov pressed on through the centre of Poland, to the south the 1st Ukrainian Front under Marshal Konev, seen here taking a look at the German forward positions through a screen of branches, was driving forward along the Kielce–Radomsk–Breslau axis to take the Silesian industrial basin.

Legend:
- FRONT LINE ON JANUARY 12 1945
- FRONT LINE ON FEBRUARY 6
- FRONT LINE ON APRIL 16
- 1ST PHASE RUSSIAN ATTACKS
- 2ND PHASE RUSSIAN ATTACKS
- FRONT BOUNDARIES
- GERMAN RETREATS
- ARMY GROUP BOUNDARIES
- ARMY BOUNDARIES
- GERMAN POCKETS
- UPPER SILESIAN INDUSTRIAL BASIN

◁ *Germany invaded: the conquest of East Prussia by the 2nd and 3rd Belorussian Fronts, and the advance of the 1st Belorussian and 1st Ukrainian Fronts from the Vistula to the Oder.*

▽ *With the Russians on the Oder, only 50 miles from Berlin, the Russians were now truly hammering at the gate with the dit-dit-dit-dah of the opening of Beethoven's 5th Symphony, used by Allied propagandists as it is also V in morse.*
▽ ▽ *Hitler and Goebbels are swept out of southern Poland by a broom of Russian bayonets.*

opposite number that Eisenhower could not "solve his problem" without prior information, albeit not detailed, of *Stavka*'s plans. As we see, this telegram of Churchill's dated January 6 did not look like an S.O.S.

4th *Panzerarmee* defeated

From January 12 to 15, the Soviet offensive extended from the Baranów bridgehead on the Vistula to Tilsit on the Niemen, finally covering a front of 750 miles. On D-day the Baranów bridgehead was 37 miles deep and held by XLVIII Panzer Corps, part of the 4th *Panzerarmee*. It had three weak infantry divisions (the 68th, 168th, and 304th) strung out along a front twice as long as it would normally cover. Each division was down to six battalions, having each had to give up one to form a corps reserve.

Corps reserve had in addition 30 tank destroyers and one company of 14 self-propelled 8.8-cm guns.

Some 12 miles from the front, in the area of Kielce–Pińczów, was the O.K.H. reserve: XXIV Panzer Corps (General Nehring: 16th and 17th Panzer Divisions). Harpe had opposed, to the best of his ability, the positioning of this unit so near to the front line, but Hitler had stuck to his decision, refusing to believe that the Soviet tanks could cover 12 miles in a day, such an idea smacking of defeatism in his opinion. And so Harpe and Gräser (4th *Panzerarmee*) must not be allowed to use up this precious reserve too soon. Like Rommel during "Overlord" they were expressly forbidden to engage it without a formal order from the Führer. Now Hitler was at Ziegenberg near Giessen and, as usual, unobtainable before 1100 hours.

Marshal Konev had ten armies, including three tank, plus three independent tank corps and three or four divisions of artillery. He had formed a first echelon of 34 infantry divisions and 1,000 tanks which he pushed into the bridgehead, giving him at the centre of gravity of the attack a superiority of 11 to 1 in infantry, 7 to 1 in tanks, and 20 to 1 in guns and mortars.

At 0300 hours on January 12, the Russians started their preparatory fire on the German positions: this stopped an hour later, and the Russians then made a decoy attack which drew the fire of XLVIII Panzer Corps and revealed the position of the German batteries. The Russians, with 320 guns per mile, then crushed the German guns with a con-

centration of unprecendented violence. Zero hour for the infantry and tanks was 1030 hours: two waves of tanks followed by three waves of infantry set out to mop up the pockets of resistance left behind by the T-34's and the JS's. They were supported by self-propelled guns firing over open sights.

By early afternoon the tanks had overrun the German gun positions and destroyed the few left after the morning shelling. By nightfall they had covered between nine and 15 miles; they carried on in spite of the darkness.

In less than 24 hours the 4th *Panzerarmee* had suffered a strategic as well as a tactical defeat, as Konev threw into the

▽ *The German night sky is lit up by a Russian* Katyusha *rocket barrage. Though not particularly accurate, the barrage fired by a* Katyusha *battery could blanket an area with as much explosive as three or four field artillery regiments' concentrated fire.*

breach his 3rd Guards Tank Army (Colonel-General Rybalko) and 4th Guards Tank Army (Colonel-General Lelyushenko), with the task of cutting off the Germans retreating from Radom and Kielce when they had crossed the Pilica. He sent his 5th Guards Army (General A. S. Zhadov) towards Czestochowa and set Kraków and the upper Silesia industrial basin as the objectives of the armies of his left.

9th Army cut to shreds

On January 14, it was the turn of Zhukov and his 1st Belorussian Front to come into the battle. The Soviet 33rd and 69th Armies (respectively under Generals V. D. Zvetayev and V. J. Kolpakchy) ran into two German divisions as they broke out of the Puławy bridgehead. The 5th Shock Army (General N. E. Berzarin) and the 8th Guards Army (General V. I. Chuikov) found themselves facing three as they in their turn advanced from the Magnuszew bridgehead. Thus, by evening on D-day the German 9th Army was broken up for good, cut to pieces even. This allowed the Russians to loose the 1st and 2nd Guards Tank Armies (Colonel-General M. E. Katukov and Colonel-General S. I. Bogdanov), sending the former off along the axis Kutno–Poznań and the latter along the axis Gostynin–Inowrocław–Hohensalza.

Chernyakhovsky's offensive

On January 13 and 14, the 2nd and 3rd Belorussian Fronts, supported by the 4th and 1st Air Armies (Generals K. A. Vershinin and T. T. Khriukin), attacked the German Army Group "Centre". In this duel between Marshal Rokossovsky and General Chernyakhovsky and Colonel-General Reinhardt, the Russians used 100 divisions, giving them a superiority of three to one. Even so, the battle raged for two days, in stark contrast to what had happened on the Vistula. General A. V. Gorbatov, commander of the Soviet 3rd Army, who had the job of driving the Germans out of their positions in the Pultusk area on the Narew, has left an account of the bitterness of the fighting: on the opening day, in spite of an "initial barrage of un-

precedented violence" he had only advanced "three to seven kilometres in the main direction, two to three the secondary direction and one to one and a half during the night's fighting". On January 14 in particular, Gorbatov had to face furious counter-attacks by the "Grossdeutschland" Panzer Corps which he describes as follows:

"A struggle of unparalleled violence and ferocity developed on the second day: this too was foggy. The enemy threw in all his reserves plus his 'Grossdeutschland' Panzer Division (sic). The latter had been on the southern frontier of East Prussia in the area of Willenberg, and our Intelligence service had failed to pick them up. Taking advantage of the fog, within 24 hours it had concentrated in the area of the break-through with the task of re-establishing the situation in our army sector, then in that of the nearest formation on our left. We had decided to attack again at 0900 hours, but the enemy prevented us. At 0820 he laid down an artillery barrage with 23 batteries of guns and 17 batteries of mortars, some six-tube *Nebelwerfers* and some heavy howitzers. At 0830 he then counter-attacked the troops which had got through into his defences. In two hours seven counter-attacks were driven off. At mid-day the German Panzer division came into action. By evening we had had 37 counter-attacks. Fighting died down only at nightfall."

On the other leg of the right-angle formed by Army Group "Centre", Chernyakhovsky's efforts were concentrated on the Schlossberg–Ebenrode front. He broke into the 3rd *Panzerarmee*'s positions but, against Germans now fighting on their own soil, was unable to

△ *Soviet commanders. From left to right these are Lieutenant-General K. F. Telegin, the third member of the military council of the 1st Belorussian Front with Zhukov and Colonel-General M. S. Malinin, the chief-of-staff; Colonel-General V. I. Chuikov, head of the 8th Guards Army; and Lieutenant-General M. I. Kazakov, head of the 69th Army. The military council was a peculiarly Russian concept: all major orders at front and army level had to be signed by the three members of the military council of the formation in question. The council consisted of the commander, his chief-of-staff, and a political member. This last was an army commissar or civilian party member. After October 1942 the political member was given a military rank.*

achieve anything like the successes won by Zhukov and Konev in Poland, where they were now exploiting their early victories.

New conflict between Hitler and Guderian

On January 16, Hitler finally abandoned what Guderian called his "little Vosges war" and returned to his office in the Chancellery. Here he made two decisions which brought a show-down with the O.K.H. Chief-of-Staff. First of all he stuck to his order to transfer the "Grossdeutschland" Panzer Corps from Army Group "Centre" to Army Group "A" and send it over to Kielce, where it was to attack the flank of the Russian tank forces advancing on Poznań. Guderian repeated the arguments he had put forward the previous evening on the phone, but in vain.

"They would not arrive in time to stop the Russians and they would be withdrawn from the defences of East Prussia at a time when the Russian offensive was reaching its peak. The loss of this formation would give rise to the same catastrophe in East Prussia as we had had on the Vistula. Whilst we were struggling for a final outcome, the divisions up to full fighting strength would still be on the trains: the 'Grossdeutschland' Panzergrenadier and the Luftwaffe 'Hermann Göring' Panzer Division of the 'Grossdeutschland' Panzer Corps, under General von Saucken, the staunchest of commanders."

It was no good, as usual, and events bore out the gloomiest of forecasts: not only did the German 2nd Army cave in and Rokossovsky set off for Elbing as ordered, but the "Grossdeutschland" Panzer Corps arrived at Lódź under a hail of Soviet shelling and only saved its neck by a prompt retreat. Reduced to a moving pocket, together with XXIV Panzer Corps, it nevertheless managed to filter back through the Soviet columns and to cross over to the left bank of the Oder.

▽ *Soviet M1942 76.2-mm gun in action. This was the standard Russian divisional artillery weapon, and could be used either as a conventional weapon or as an anti-tank gun. Compared with equivalent British and American weapons, the 25-pounder and 75-mm, which had ranges of 13,400 and 13,600 yards, the Russian gun had the considerably better range of 15,000 yards.*

Hitler may have satisfied Guderian's demand by announcing that he would go over to the defensive on the Western Front, but he aroused his indignation by ordering to Hungary the best of the formations salvaged in this manner, in particular the 6th S.S. *Panzerarmee*. In Guderian's opinion, the Hungarian railways could not cope with the traffic and it would take weeks before Army Group "South" could go over to the counter-attack as Hitler had ordered, whereas Sepp Dietrich's Panzers could concentrate on the Oder in ten days. Beaten on the military question, the Führer counter-attacked on the grounds of the economy, maintaining "that Hungarian petroleum deposits and the nearby refineries are indispensable after the bombing of the German coal hydrogenation plants, and have become decisively important for the conduct of the war. No more fuel means your tanks can't run or your planes take off. You must see that. But that's the way it is: my generals understand nothing of the economy of war!"

Hitler's reasoning was clearly not devoid of foundation as petroleum, until uranium came along, was the life-blood of war. But his chief-of-staff's calculations turned out to be correct, since the 6th *Panzerarmee* had to wait until March 6 before it could launch its offensive on the Hungarian front. Even so, its intervention north of the Carpathians was hardly likely to have prevented Zhukov from reaching the Oder between Küstrin and Frankfurt. Diverting it to the south made the Soviet invasion easier.

Changes in the German command

The catastrophe in Poland demanded a scapegoat. Hitler chose one in the person of Colonel-General Harpe, C.-in-C. Army Group "A", forgetting that he had himself ordered the imprudent stationing of XXIV Panzer Corps in O.K.H. reserve very close to Harpe's lines. This was the root of the trouble, as Hitler realised, but only after dismissing Harpe's warnings.

Harpe was replaced by Colonel-General Schörner, and Rendulic, Schörner's colleague, received command of Army Group "North", which had just driven off strong Soviet attacks in the Kurland bridgehead. Scarcely had Rendulic left Oslo, received

△ *Colonel-General P. S. Rybalko* (seated), *commander of the 3rd Guards Tank Army, follows the progress of his forces, part of Konev's 1st Ukrainian Front.*

the Swords to his Knight's Cross from Hitler, and unpacked his bags in his new command post than on January 26 he received the order to go to East Prussia and take over immediately the command of Army Group "Centre". Unfortunately for this group, in spite of the valour of its new commander, nothing could be done to stave off the impending disaster.

Hitler at fault again

It cannot, of course, be argued that Reinhardt could have forced Rokossovsky and Chernyakhovsky to give up their offensive if he had had the use of the *"Grossdeutschland"* Panzer Corps. There is no doubt, however, that by depriving him of this formation, Hitler virtually condemned Army Group "Centre" to inescapable defeat, a defeat which reached the proportions of a strategic catastrophe, involving the total destruction of 28 German divisions.

In planning the offensive, *Stavka* had given the 3rd Belorussian Front the task of destroying the enemy forces in Tilsit and Insterburg, then of making for Königsberg. The 2nd Belorussian Front was to overcome the enemy resistance in the Przasnysz–Mława area and then

The German 10.5-cm *Sturmhaubitze* 42 *Ausf.* G assault howitzer

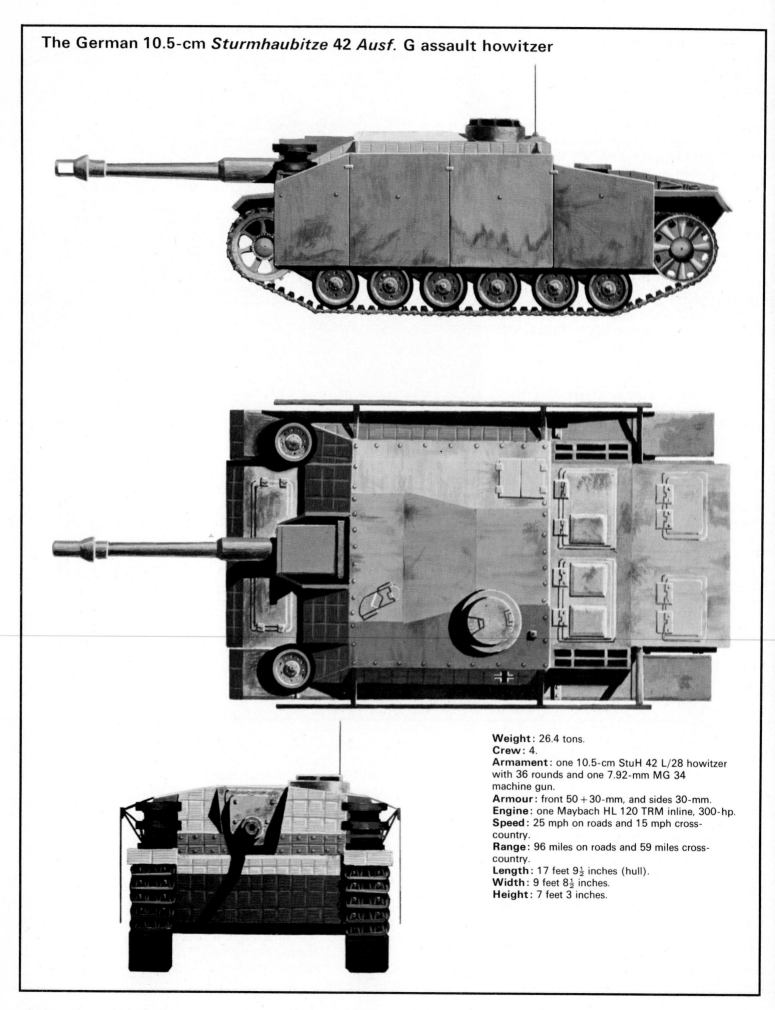

Weight: 26.4 tons.
Crew: 4.
Armament: one 10.5-cm StuH 42 L/28 howitzer with 36 rounds and one 7.92-mm MG 34 machine gun.
Armour: front 50 + 30-mm, and sides 30-mm.
Engine: one Maybach HL 120 TRM inline, 300-hp.
Speed: 25 mph on roads and 15 mph cross-country.
Range: 96 miles on roads and 59 miles cross-country.
Length: 17 feet 9½ inches (hull).
Width: 9 feet 8½ inches.
Height: 7 feet 3 inches.

The Russian KV-85 heavy tank

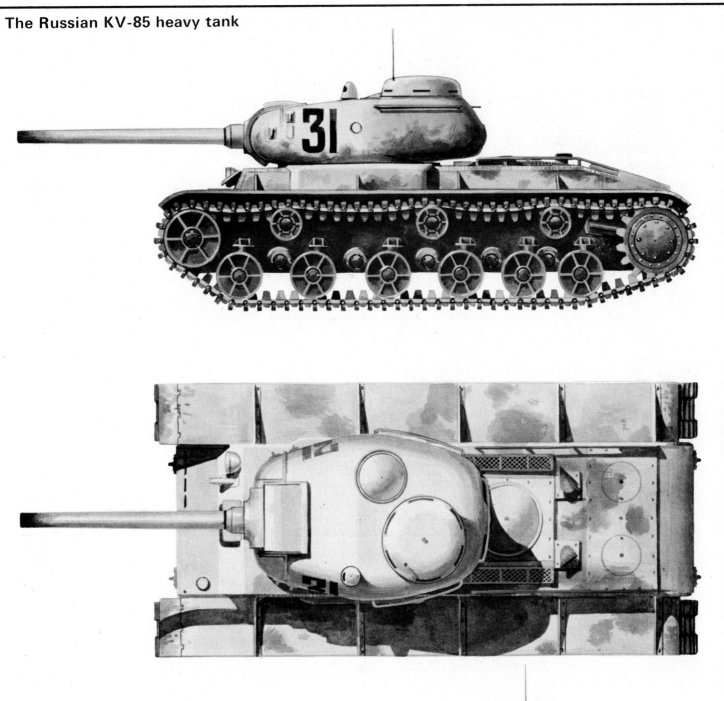

Weight: 45 tons.
Crew: 5.
Armament: one 85-mm M1944 gun with 71
rounds and three 7.62-mm DT machine guns
with 3,276 rounds.
Armour: hull nose and front 75-mm, sides 65-mm,
and rear 60-mm; turret front, sides, and rear
110-mm, and mantlet 95-mm.
Engine: one V-2K inline, 600-hp.
Speed: 25 mph.
Range: 205 miles.
Length: 22 feet 6 inches
Width: 11 feet 4 inches.
Height: 10 feet 10 inches.

advance along the axis Deutsch-Eylau–Marienburg–Elbing. This would prevent the Germans driven out by Chernyakhovsky from crossing the Vistula, and they would then fall into the hands of Rokossovsky. Apart from slight variations this was the manoeuvre attempted by Rennenkampf and Samsonov in August 1914 against East Prussia, which ended up in their defeat at Tannenberg and the Masurian Lakes. Here, however, all resemblance between the two campaigns ceases. Chernyakhovsky and Rokossovsky were younger and more energetic than their predecessors in the Tsar's army. Trammelled by the despotic authority of the Führer, Reinhardt on his side had none of that perfect freedom of action which Colonel-General von Hindenburg enjoyed under the Kaiser and Moltke.

Rokossovsky reaches East Prussia

In spite of the German 2nd Army's resistance, the 2nd Belorussian Front's attack began again on January 16, favoured by a bright spell which allowed efficient support by General Vershinin's planes. Two days later the Russian forward troops were engaged some 21 miles from their point of departure, in the area of Przasnysz and Ciéchanow. Forty-eight hours later Rokossovsky took Mława and Dzialdowo (Soldau), reached the East Prussian frontier, which he then crossed, and launched his 5th Tank Army towards its objective at Elbing. From then on things moved quickly, and Hitler only just had time to blow up the monument to the German victory at Tannenberg and to have the mortal remains of Field-Marshal von Hindenburg and his wife exhumed and evacuated.

On the same day the 3rd Belorussian Front had overcome the 3rd *Panzerarmee,* which finally succumbed on January 19. By the 21st, the Russians had taken the fortified position along the Inster, with the little town of Insterburg, and Tilsit, where Lieutenant-General Rein's 69th Division had held out, almost to the last grenadier, Rein himself sharing the fate of his men. A few days later Chernyakhovsky had his right at Labiau, at the edge of the frozen lagoon of the Kurisches Haff, his centre at Wehlau, on the west bank of the Alle less than 31 miles from Königsberg, and his left from Gołdap to Lyck in the Masurian Lakes area.

The trap closes on Army Group "Centre"

On January 17, when it became clear that Rokossovsky's battering-ram would destroy his 2nd Army, Reinhardt had asked permission to pull back the 4th Army from its 140-mile wide front (Nowogród–Augustów–Gołdap) to a line Ortelsburg–Lötzen – Masurian Lakes canal. This would save three divisions, which would make up for the loss of the *"Grossdeutschland"* Panzer Corps and stave off a break-through. Quoting his "five years experience of warfare", Hitler refused this sensible request; Reinhardt could not bring himself to remind Hitler of the sinister experience of Vitebsk.

Three days later, when the German 2nd Army positions had been breached and Chernyakhovsky had been successful at Tilsit on the Inster, Lieutenant-General Heidkämper, chief-of-staff of Army Group "Centre", noted in his diary: "To keep the 4th Army in its present exposed position now appears grotesque. At 2030 hours the C.-in-C. (Reinhardt) again puts before the Führer the reasons for its immediate withdrawal. *'Mein Führer'*, he began, 'in my anxiety for the safety of East Prussia, I venture again to turn to you. According to my appreciation of the situation, we shall tomorrow face an attack on the whole of East Prussia. Examination of a captured map reveals that the 5th Guards Tank Army, with four tank corps, is to make for Danzig. The strength of our 2nd Army is so depleted that we cannot withstand this attack. The second strategic danger is in the 3rd *Panzerarmee,* which the enemy has broken into. If the Guards Tank Army is able to force its way through we shall be caught in the rear: here we have no resources at all.'"

There followed long exchanges between Reinhardt and Hitler. The latter, never short of arguments, advised Reinhardt to use the *Volkssturm* militia against the Soviet tanks and told him that the 4th Panzer Division had been withdrawn from Kurland, loaded on five liners, and was expected to reach him very soon. This would be followed very shortly by 20 infantry battalions from Denmark. It

was for these reasons that he opposed Reinhardt's request, and when at mid-day on January 21 he finally agreed, the fate of Army Group "Centre" had been sealed.

By remaining in its allotted positions on January 17, 4th Army suffered the inevitable encirclement, with 350,000 men trapped around the strongpoint of Lötzen, where supplies were reckoned to be enough for one division for 70 days. The commander, General Hossbach, realising the impossibility of his position, tried to fight his way out, down towards the Vistula. He was thus knowingly disobeying O.K.H.'s orders, but he had the approval of Colonel-General Reinhardt, who saw in this a chance of saving the 3rd *Panzerarmee* as well.

Holding off Chernyakhovsky on the line Sensburg – Rastenburg – Friedland – left bank of the Pregel, Hossbach, after 125 miles of forced marches in five days through snowstorms, nevertheless failed to get to Elbing before the Soviet 5th Guards Tank Army. The latter had reached the shore of the Frisches Haff near the little town of Tolkemit on

◁ *A German officer, clad in a snow-suit, finds it heavy going in the winter snows of 1944-45.*
▽ *However, the cold still managed to take its tithe of the exhausted German forces.*

January 27 and had cut the last link between East Prussia and the rest of the Reich. Further south, XXVI and VI Corps (Generals Matzky and Grossmann) had attacked the previous night and got as far as Preussisch-Holland, 12 miles south of Elbing.

On the one hand Rokossovsky was thus able to avoid the opposition intended for him and consequently to reinforce his strength. On the other the secret evacuation of East Prussia by Hossbach, with the connivance of Reinhardt, was denounced to Hitler by Erich Koch, the *Gauleiter* of the province. The Führer dreaded the setting up in Königsberg of a government of "Free Germany" once the Russians were in the town. It was here that Frederick I, the Elector of Brandendurg, had been crowned in 1701. It therefore had to be held at any price, even at the cost of 28 divisions.

And so Reinhardt was relieved by Rendulic on January 27. Three days later Hossbach was ordered to hand over command of the 4th Army to General Friedrich-Wilhelm Müller. Stalin had, of course, no intention of setting up a Free German Government (even one devoted to him and presided over by General von Seydlitz-Kurzbach) in Königsberg, which had been allotted to the Soviet Union by the Teheran Conference, and which he was going to rename Kaliningrad. Was this just mistrust on Stalin's part, or did he think it best to leave things as they were?

The Russians gather momentum

Whilst the ring was closing round the 3rd *Panzerarmee* and the 4th Army, and what was left of the 2nd Army was powerless to prevent the forces of the 2nd Belorussian Front from crossing the lower Vistula, Colonel-General Schörner's savage energy was unable to hold back the onrush of Marshals Zhukov and Konev, though their losses, the strain on their equipment, and the stretching of their lines of communication eventually slowed the Russians down to advances of less than half a mile in places.

On January 15, between the Baranów bridgehead and the Carpathians, the 4th Ukrainian Front came into action with 18 infantry divisions and two tank corps. At Jaslo it easily broke through the thinly-held line of the 1st *Panzerarmee* and set off for Kraków without hindrance.

On January 16, Guderian noted, the Russian advance "gathered extraordinary speed". In effect, on the 1st Belorussian Front the 4th Tank Army, having passed through Jedrzejów the night before, reached Czestochowa on the 17th in two stages, covering a total distance of 70 miles. On its right the 3rd Guards Tank Army reached Radomsko from Kielce (50 miles). It was therefore to be concluded that all organised resistance had ceased in front of Lelyushenko's and Rybalko's forces.

Kraków falls to Konev

This explains how Konev was able to take Kraków by an outflanking movement, so that on January 19 the Poles found it left virtually intact. The same procedure, in an operation which he

▽ *Cossack cavalry stop to water their mounts . . .*

shared equally with Petrov's 4th Ukrainian Front, gave him the industrial labyrinth of upper Silesia with its factories only slightly damaged. And, a more difficult task, he had managed to prevent the Germans from sabotaging them.

The ruins of Warsaw abandoned

On the 1st Belorussian Front the advance proceeded at an equally fast pace. On January 16 Zhukov's right having seized Modlin, where the Bug joins the Vistula, the Warsaw garrison of four incomplete battalions and a few artillery batteries sought and obtained O.K.H.'s approval to abandon the ruins of the city and escape encirclement. This common-sense decision put Hitler in a state of indescribable fury. In spite of Guderian's vehement protests, he arrested three officers of the operations staff and had Guderian himself undergo a wearisome interrogation by Kaltenbrunner.

By January 19, the 1st and 2nd Guards Tank Armies had reached their first objectives. Konev advanced from Gostynin to Inowrocław then to Bydgoszcz (Bromberg). On January 23, having covered 90 miles in four days, he occupied the latter without resistance. On the left, Colonel-General Bogdanov took a week to cover the 110 miles from Kutno to Poznań. The old fortress of Poznań, dating back to the Prussian era, had been hastily re-armed and put under the command of Major-General Mattern. The 2nd Guards Tank Army had better things to do, and so by-passed it and drove on: next stop Frankfurt on the Oder.

On the same day, the left of the 1st Belorussian Front took Łódz, and south of it advanced to make contact with the 1st Ukrainian Front. Remnants of retreating German units of Army Group "A" mingled with the advancing Russians. "The enemy," Guderian said, "had virtually nothing in front of him. Only the moving pockets of XXIV and the 'Grossdeutschland' Panzer Corps moved on westwards, fighting all the time, imperturbable, picking up a host of smaller units as they went along. Generals Nehring and von Saucken carried out a military exploit during these days every bit worthy to be recounted by a new Xenophon."

Marshals Zhukov and Konev now had no difficulty in overcoming the resistance put up by Colonel-General Schörner to

△ . . . *leaving a burning Polish village in their wake.*

Further down the Oder, Generals Nehring and von Saucken had managed to escape from the pursuing 1st Belorussian Front and had crossed back over the river at Glogau (Głogów). Zhukov's two Guards Tank Armies covered a good 60 miles along the Poznań–Berlin axis, where two weak divisions, without artillery, had been sent to prop up what was left of the German 9th Army. Without halting at the small garrison of Schneidemühl (Piła), which they by-passed, they reached the Oder at Küstrin in the early days of February. This brought them opposite Frankfurt, around which bridgeheads on the left bank were soon established. And so Zhukov's forward troops were now only 50 miles as the crow flies from the New Chancellery bunker.

The German hecatomb

On the 30th day of the offensive, Moscow published the first figures from Konev's and Zhukov's victories: 70 German divisions destroyed or cut to pieces; 295,000 men killed and 86,000 taken prisoner; 15,000 guns and mortars, 34,000 vehicles, and 2,955 tanks destroyed or captured. If it is realised that the mobile reserves behind Army Group "A" consisted of five Panzer and two *Panzergrenadier* divisions, the last figure seems to bear no relation to reality. As for the ratio of killed to prisoners, as Alexander Werth has pointed out, it belies the statements of the Soviet propagandist Ilya Ehrenburg, who described to his readers "Germans running away like rabbits". And Werth also recalls the confidential statement of an officer from the front who said to him "In some places their resistance reminds me of Sebastopol: those German soldiers can be quite heroic at times."

At the same time, Zhukov was in front of Küstrin and 335 miles from his point of departure, whilst Konev in Silesia was 300 miles from his. Logistic considerations now became of prime importance to the two marshals' tank armies, especially as they had greatly outdistanced the infantry following them on foot. And so February, March, and early April were devoted to small-scale operations only, though these were important as they led to the mopping up of East Prussia and the deployment of the Red Army on what is now called the Oder-Neisse line, ready for the final offensive.

△ *A column of Russian T-34/85 medium tanks arrives in Heiligenbeil, on the Frisches Haff, only about 25 miles from Königsberg.*

slow their advance. On January 18, the 72nd Division was wiped out near Piotrków, then the 10th Panzer, 78th, and 291st Divisions succumbed trying to block the way into Silesia to the Soviet tanks. They were no more of an obstacle than the Oder would be. By the end of January the forward troops of the 1st Ukrainian Front had reached the Oder above Oppeln (Opole) and on either side of Breslau (Wrocław) had established two vast bridgeheads at Brieg (Brzeg) and Steinau (Scinawa) on the right bank. This marked the beginning of the encirclement of the Silesian capital.

CHAPTER 143
Advance to the Oder

Marshal Rokossovsky's break-through towards Elbing and the crushing defeat of the German 2nd Army (which was driven back to Danzig) left the left wing of Army Group "A" uncovered, and west of a line running north-south through Toruń the whole of Pomerania lay open to the Soviet invader. In mid-January there was little more than a handful of troops, mostly infantry, to defend it.

To close this enormous breach, Guderian got Hitler to approve the formation of an Army Group "Vistula", but the two men were violently opposed on the question of who was to command it. The reshuffling of commands in the Danube theatre meant that the general staff of Army Group "F" were out of jobs, as also was Field-Marshal von Weichs, whom Guderian described as "a man who is as intelligent as he is brave and upright and one certainly cut out to master such a difficult situation, insofar as it can be mastered." But Weich's profound religious feelings disqualified him in Hitler's eyes. So, despite Guderian's violent protests, this delicate command was given to *Reichsführer*-S.S. Heinrich Himmler. Himmler had no religious feelings, to be sure, but during Operation *"Nordwind"* in lower Alsace he had shown both ineptitude and hesitation in command. What was worse, Hitler refused Guderian's proposal that the staff of Army Group "F" should come under his control. Himmler was thus able to recruit his own from amongst his cronies, and as chief-of-staff he chose Lieutenant-General Lammerding of the *Waffen*-S.S.,

whose name will for ever be linked with Oradour-sur-Glane.

On January 25, Army Group "North" was renamed "Kurland", "Centre" was renamed "North", and "A" became "Centre". The general staff of the 3rd *Panzer-armee* were withdrawn from East Prussia and put under Army Group "Vistula". By emptying the depôts, schools, and training centres and sending part of Berlin's A.A. defences down to the Oder, O.K.H. was able for the last time to reconstitute some kind of coherent force with which to face the Russians.

In early February it had five army groups with a total of 135 divisions deployed as follows:

	Infantry divisions	Panzer and *Panzer-grenadier* divisions	*Totals*
"Kurland"	20	2	22
"North"	19	5	24
"Vistula"	25	8	33
"Centre"	20	8	28
"South"	19	9	28
Totals	103	32	135

Surrender in the West?

In less than a month, in spite of the reinforcements we have mentioned, the number of German divisions facing the Red Army had dropped from 164 to 135. Most of these were below strength and some were down to the equivalent of an

▽ *Russian bridge-builders at work in the Oder. Only with the completion of a heavy duty bridge could the bridgehead on the west bank be considered at all secure. Note the considerably more primitive, yet nevertheless effective, construction methods of the Russians compared with the Western Allies.*

infantry regiment. Under these circumstances, Guderian understandably thought that Ribbentrop should be informed of the situation. He suggested that the two of them should approach Hitler to recommend that Germany lay down her arms in the West. Ribbentrop was unwilling, so Guderian attempted to win Hitler over to a manoeuvre which, for some weeks at least, would avert the threat to Berlin.

"I resolved," he said, "to demonstrate once more to Hitler that the Hungarian offensive had to be abandoned. Instead we would attack the Russian salient on the Oder between Frankfurt and Küstrin by going for its flanks, which were not very strong, in the south on the line Glogau–Guben and in the north of the line Pyritz–Arnswalde. I thus hoped to strengthen the defence of the capital and the interior of the Reich and gain time to conclude armistice talks with the Western powers."

But this proposal, which presupposed the evacuation also of Kurland, Norway, and Italy, merely provoked Hitler to an attack of maniacal fury.

▽ *Polish refugees arrive back in Graudenz after its liberation by the Russians.*

Russian superiority overwhelming

As the 6th *Panzerarmee* finally set off for Hungary, Guderian's proposed pincer round the tank armies of the 1st Belorussian Front became impossible through lack of resources. He therefore fell back on a flank attack which was to bring into operation Army Group "Vistula". Breaking out south-east from Arnswalde, it would beat the enemy forces north of the Warta, which would protect Pomerania and force Zhukov to give up his positions before Frankfurt and Küstrin. Speed was essential, but Himmler and his staff took a week to get ready. Konev's vigorous attacks in Silesia, moreover, obliged O.K.H. to reinforce Army Group "Centre" at the expense of Army Group "Vistula".

On February 13, the 3rd *Panzerarmee* finally mounted a counter-attack, starting from Arnswalde, and scored some initial success. But it was soon compelled to go

over to the defensive, as *Stavka* turned on to it Rokossovsky's centre and left as well as Zhukov's two tank armies. With his left at Könitz and his right on the Oder at Schwedt, Colonel-General Raus was defending a front of 160 miles with only eight divisions. It is therefore not surprising that this was quickly broken by the two Soviet marshals' offensive on February 24. They had nine tank corps and no fewer than 47 infantry divisions.

Back to the Baltic

Driving on through Schlochau and Büblitz, the 2nd Belorussian Front's tanks reached the Baltic north of Köslin on February 28, cutting the German 2nd Army's last land communications with the rest of the Reich. This army now had its back to the sea, its right on the Stolpe and its left on the Nogat. A few days later Zhukov broke through to Dramburg and drove on to Treptow, in spite of the

intervention one after the other of four Panzer or *Panzergrenadier* divisions. During this fighting General Krappe's X S.S. Panzer Corps was wiped out and Raus was just able to save some 50,000 men of his army who, on March 11, were sheltering on Wolin Island. Eight days later a special Kremlin communiqué announced the capture of the port of Kolberg (now Kołobrzeg) where the 163rd and the 402nd Divisions were cut to pieces almost to the last man.

△ *German corpses litter the pavements of Brieg after its capture by the 1st Ukrainian Front. From here the southern arm of a pincer would sweep up to close the trap around Breslau.*

Konev invades Silesia

Konev's job in Silesia was to align his front with Zhukov's, according to Russian official histories today. But was it to be only this? Judging by the means employed, it seems unlikely.

On February 4, Konev launched a first attack when he broke out of the bridgehead at Brieg and advanced nearly 13 miles along the left bank of the Oder. South-east of Breslau, the Russians advanced as far as Ohlan, some 13 miles from the Silesian capital, and south down to Strehlen. A special Moscow communiqué claimed that this action brought in 4,200 prisoners.

△ *The wreckage of a Messerschmitt Bf 110 unit of the Luftwaffe, caught by a surprise Russian attack.*

A week later the 3rd Guards Tank and the 4th Tank Armies broke out from the Steinau bridgehead and advanced at Blitzkrieg speed over the plain of Silesia. On February 13, Colonel-General Lelyushenko was attacking Glogau, 25 miles north-west of Steinau. On his left, supported by a division of artillery and followed by Colonel-General K. A. Koroteev's 52nd Army, Rokossovsky had forced a crossing of the Bober at Bunzlau the night before. On February 15, after a 60-mile dash north-west, the Soviet tanks reached Guben, Sommerfeld, Sorau, and Sagan, which they lost and regained in circumstances still unknown.

So Konev's aim was not merely to align his front with Zhukov's but to cross the Neisse, roll up the front along the Oder down-river from Fürstenberg, and advance towards Berlin through Cottbus. Halted on the Neisse, either by *Stavka* or by enemy opposition, however, he closed the ring round Breslau. At the beginning of March, he was facing Schörner on the line Bunzlau – Jauer – Schweidnitz – Neisse – Ratibor, at the foot of the mountains separating Silesia from Bohemia and Moldavia.

Mopping up East Prussia fell to the 3rd Belorussian Front, reinforced up to 100 divisions against the 24, including five Panzer, of Army Group "North", at the beginning of February. At the same date the Russians were in the outskirts of

Königsberg; from here the front moved along the course of the river Alle between Friedland and Guttstadt, then turned north-west to reach the coast near Frauenberg. This left the Germans trapped in a rectangle about the size of Brighton – Guildford – Winchester – Portsmouth. Colonel-General Rendulic did not limit himself merely to defensive operations. On February 19 he counterattacked in a pincer manoeuvre and re-established communication, though precariously, between Königsberg and Pillau, the latter a Baltic port giving him a supply and evacuation link with the rest of the Reich less exposed than Königsberg.

Chernyakhovsky's idea had been to cut East Prussia in two from south-west to north-east, but on February 18 he was killed in front of Mehlsack by a shell splinter as he was on his way to the H.Q. of General Gorbatov, commander of the 3rd Army. Twice decorated a Hero of the Soviet Union, he was the youngest and one of the most gifted of the great Russian war leaders. In his honour the small Prussian town of Insterburg was renamed Chernyakhovsk.

Stalin nominated Marshal A. M. Vasilevsky to succeed him, while Vasilevsky's job as Chief-of-Staff of the Red Army was taken over by General A. I. Antonov.

The offensive proceeded along the same axis, in spite of obstinate German resistance, which General Gorbatov emphasises in his memoirs. The invaders' superior strength soon began to tell, however. On March 14, the Russian 3rd Army concentrated on a narrow front twice as much infantry and five times as much artillery as the Germans, gained over three miles in three days and got to within eight miles of the sea, which it finally reached on March 25. "What a sight on the coast!" Gorbatov writes. "Several square miles of lorries and vans loaded with *matériel*, food, and domestic equipment. Between the vehicles lay corpses of German soldiers. Some 300 horses were attached in pairs to a chain and many of these were dead too."

Königsberg falls

And so the German 4th Army was cut in two and trapped in two pockets. Meanwhile, on March 12, Hitler had replaced

The Russian Joseph Stalin-2 heavy tank

Weight: 45.5 tons.
Crew: 4.
Armament: one 122-mm D-25 gun with 28 rounds, one 12.7-mm DShK and two 7.62 DT machine guns.
Armour: hull glacis 110-mm, nose 127-mm, sides 89-mm, and front pannier sides 133-mm; turret front 64-mm, sides 95-mm, roof 45-mm, and mantlet 102-mm.
Engine: one V-2K inline, 600-hp.
Speed: 27 mph.
Range: 100 miles.
Length: 31 feet 7 inches.
Width: 10 feet 3 inches.
Height: 9 feet.

Rendulic as C.-in-C. Army Group "Kurland" and Colonel-General Weiss, C.-in-C. 2nd Army, was given the sad honour of presiding over the death-throes of Army Group "North". On March 30, the pocket which had formed round the little towns of Braunsberg and Heiligenbeil surrendered, yielding (if we are to believe a Soviet communiqué of the period) 80,000 dead and 50,000 prisoners. In the night of April 9-10 General Lasch, commander of the Königsberg fortress, decided to send envoys to Marshal Vasilevsky. The town had been under heavy and incessant air bombardment for some ten days, whilst the attackers, having taken the fortifications, infiltrated the streets amidst the burning buildings. No German authors we have consulted blame the commander for surrendering, though 92,000 men were taken prisoner and 2,232 guns were lost. Lasch was condemned to death in his

absence, however, and his family imprisoned.

On April 15, the Russians invaded the Samland peninsula, from which they had been driven out two months previously. Ten days later, the last remnants of the German 4th Army, now under the command of General von Saucken, evacuated the port of Pillau, which had served as a transit station for 141,000 military wounded and 451,000 civilian refugees since January 15.

Along the lower Vistula, Rokossovsky had the right of the 2nd Belorussian Front, and in particular the Polish 2nd Army (General Swierczewski) facing the six corps and 17 divisions, all very delapidated, which the reorganisation of command in late June had put into the incapable hands of the sinister Heinrich Himmler.

By February 18, on the right

▽ *A Russian SU-152 assault gun lumbers into the ruins of Königsberg, once the heart of East Prussia.*

bank of the Vistula, the Russians had reached Graudenz (Grudziadz) but it took them until March 5 to overcome the last resistance of this small town. On February 21 they took Dirschau (Tczew) on the left bank 21 miles from Danzig. On March 9, the Soviet forces which had reached the Baltic north of Köslin crossed the Stolpe and drove on towards Kartuzy, turning the right flank of the German 2nd Army, which had come under the command of General von Saucken after the transfer of Colonel-General Rendulic.

Danzig, Gdynia, and Poznań occupied

The struggle was now concentrated around Danzig and Gdynia, which the Germans had renamed Gotenhafen. In this hopeless battle the defenders brought in the pocket-battleship *Lützow* and the cruisers *Prinz Eugen* and *Leipzig,* which several times knocked out Soviet tanks with their gunfire, though their ammunition was gradually more and more severely rationed. On March 23, the Polish 2nd Army took Sopot, half-way between Danzig and Gdynia, and by the 30th it was all over. The German 2nd Army held out obstinately until May 9 in the Hela peninsula, in the Vistula estuary, and in the narrow strip of land enclosing the Frisches Haff, so that between January 15 and April 30 no fewer than 300,000 military personnel and 962,000 civilians had been embarked for Germany.

The strongpoint of Poznań gave in on February 24 after a resistance to which the Red Army paid considerable tribute. Then it was the turn of Schneidemühl and Deutsche Krone in Pomerania.

On the Oder, the fortress of Glogau, first attacked on February 13, held out until April 2. By the latter date, apart from the coastal strips held by Saucken and the Kurland bridgehead which continued to defy the Soviet assaults, the only point still holding out east of the Oder-Neisse line was Breslau. Its garrison, commanded by Lieutenant-General Niehőff, was now closely hemmed in by the 6th Army of the 1st Ukrainian Front under General V. A. Gluzdovsky.

This military tragedy was echoed by a national tragedy unprecedented in contemporary history: the exodus of nearly eight million Germans who had taken refuge on the other side of the Oder-Neisse line at the time of the capitulation of May 8, 1945. But not all those who fled before the Soviet invasion managed to find shelter. The journalist Bernard George reckons that 1,600,000 people, mostly old men, women, and children, died of exhaustion, cold, and brutal treatment from a soldiery drunk for revenge. And so in five months, this catastrophe cost Germany more civilians than France lost soldiers in the whole of the 52 months of World War I. Much of the responsibility for this affair must naturally be laid on Hitler (and his collaborators in the government and the party) and on the party authorities in Germany's eastern provinces: *Gauleiters* Erich Koch in Eastern Prussia, Forster in Danzig and Western Prussia (the former Polish corridor), and Arthur Greiser in the Warthegau, the new German name for the provinces of Poznań, Lódź (Litzmannstadt), and Czestochowa, annexed to the Third Reich in October 1939.

Hitler had obstinately refused to consider the possibility of a Russian invasion and went into fits of furious temper when anyone dared broach the subject in his presence. All preparations, even all estimates for the evacuation of the civilian population in the threatened provinces appeared to the *Gauleiters* of Königsberg, Danzig, and Poznań a scandalous demonstration of defeatism and an intolerable attack on the dogma of the Führer's infallibility. And so in many areas the exodus was improvised actually under enemy shelling. In June 1940, when the French refugees poured out along the roads there were vehicles and petrol supplies and the weather was good. In January and February 1945, the Germans had only their animals and carts, it was snowing hard, and the temperature was 20 to 25 degrees below zero Centigrade.

In his war memoirs, Colonel-General Rendulic, who saw these pitiful convoys pass by, remarked how they were often led by French prisoners, the only able-bodied men left in the villages of East Prussia, whom the refugees praised unstintingly for their devotion. On many occasions, and this was borne out by other witnesses, they protected the women and girls from the violence of their Allies.

Much has been written in Germany about the atrocities committed by the Soviet invaders. The evidence has

△△ *An SU-76 assault gun pushes its way through the detritus of the German retreat back towards Berlin.*
△ *German dead. Against the crushing weight of Russian guns and tanks, the German Army had little or no chance.*

been doubted by some, but a Red Army officer said to Werth:

"In Poland a few regrettable things happened from time to time, but, on the whole, a fairly strict discipline was maintained as regards 'rape'. The most common offence in Poland was 'dai chasy' – 'give me your wrist-watch'. There was an awful lot of petty thieving and robbery. Our fellows were just crazy about wrist-watches – there's no getting away from it. But the looting and raping in a big way did not start until our soldiers got to Germany. Our fellows were so sex-starved that they often raped old women of sixty, or seventy or even eighty – much to these grandmother's surprise, if not downright delight. But I admit it was a nasty business, and the record of the Kazakhs and other Asiatic troops was particularly bad."

It is hardly surprising that the Soviet soldiers, after the devastation of their villages, and after just seeing the abominations of the extermination camps of Maidenek, Treblinka, and Oswiecim (or Auschwitz) should exact revenge on the German people. On the other hand, the American, British, and French troops who discovered Ravensbrück, Bergen-Belsen, Buchenwald, and Dachau seem to have reacted differently. It would appear that neither the military nor the political authorities, normally so strict in matters of discipline, took the trouble at the time to stem this tide of bestiality. Very much to the contrary, journalists and intellectuals such as the well-known Ilya Ehrenburg incited the Red Army in the press and on the radio to dishonour their victory. And this homicidal propaganda cannot but have had the approval of the Kremlin. On April 14, as Alexander Werth reported, there was a sudden change of tone: Ehrenburg was brutally disowned in an official-looking article in *Pravda* by Comrade G. F. Alexandrov, then the licensed ideologist of the Central Committee of the Communist Party of the U.S.S.R. His "clumsy error" was not to have noticed that Stalin had just proclaimed: "Hitlers come and go, but the German people go on for ever."

It seems that the Kremlin feared that the horrors caused by the invasion might prevent the free flowering of communism in Central Europe. That was right, but it was too late.